THE CAT...
Wedding
Book

A complete guidebook for brides, grooms and their parents, with instructions for planning the ritual, managing people and details in the best possible style, and keeping a sense of humor when everyone else is panicking.

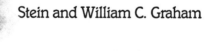

Stein and William C. Graham

Paulist Press ♥ *New York* ♥ *Mahwah*

Book design by Theresa M. Sparacio.

The English translation of the *Rite of Marriage* is copyrighted © 1969 by the International Committee on English in the Liturgy, Inc. All rights reserved. Scripture texts used in this work are taken from the *New American Bible*, copyright © 1970 by the Confraternity of Christian Doctrine, Washington, D.C., and are used by license of said copyright owner. No part of the *New American Bible* may be reproduced in any form without permission in writing. All rights reserved.

Illustrations by Ray Burns.

Library of Congress Cataloging-in-Publication Data

Stein , Molly K., 1953-
    The Catholic wedding book / by Molly K. Stein and William C Graham.
      p. cm.
    ISBN 0-8091-2956-6 (pbk.)
    1. Marriage service.   2. Weddings.   3. Catholic Church—Liturgy.
I. Graham, William C., 1950-   II. Title
BX2250.S74   1988
265'.5—dc19   88-2390
                                           CIP

Published by Paulist Press
997 Macarthur Boulevard
Mahwah, New Jersey 07430

Printed and bound in the
United States of America

Contents

Part II
Behind the Scenes

Part III
Beyond the Footlights

DEDICATED
TO THE MEMORY OF
PAUL FRANCIS ANDERSON
THE FIFTH BISHOP OF DULUTH
WHO LOVED AND TAUGHT HIS PEOPLE WELL

Acknowledgements

We are grateful to
the brides and grooms,
our priest friends and associates
Paul Stein,
and our families and friends
who have challenged us
to grow in patience,
in wisdom
and in holiness.

What has been is what will be,
and what has been done is what will be done;
and there is nothing new under the sun.

—Ecclesiastes 1:9

And he who sat upon the throne said,
'Behold, I make all things new.'

—Revelation 21:5

A Wedding Prayer

Good and gracious God,
giver of all gifts,
you have given us the sacrament of marriage
so that man and woman might live together in love
and be for us a sign of your far greater
and most perfect love.
Hear our prayer today
for those who enter marriage:
make them healthy and happy and holy
all the days of their lives,
both today and forever
with Jesus, our Christ and our Brother

Amen!

A Wedding Blessing

May the Lord
who lives in light
come near your lives
with the undying brilliance
of his radiant love.

May the Lord
who does not diminish
as shadows bring the night
protect you
under his eagle wing.

May he give you
the strength to be gentle
and the will to be kind.

May he make holy
the moments and the years
of your love,
enriching you always
with family and with friends

May he open your hearts
to his word
and, at last, when you come to rest,
may he give you unending peace,
the Father,
the Son, and
the Holy Spirit.
Amen!

(Adapted from John R. Roach's
blessing over the city of St. Paul at
his installation as archbishop)

A Letter

Dear Bride and Groom,

The time has come, the Walrus said, to talk of many things.

There are indeed many things to talk over as you prepare to exchange your vows within a Catholic ceremony. Whether you plan to be surrounded by a few close friends and family members or as many guests as the fire marshal will allow, there are important decisions to be made. The details can be so numerous that they threaten to overshadow the importance of the occasion. Often you might wish for the flick of a magic wand that will bring happily ever after to instant reality.

During these festive months of preparation for your wedding day and married life, examine who you are and hope to become. Look closely at what you are about. Try to understand both the nuances and the impact of the preparation for and celebration of your wedding. Let your preparation be a model for the life you are beginning together.

Our fond hope is that this book will help you as you think of these many things, and that it will assist you in celebrating your wedding with confidence—and fun!

May the gracious God who has begun this good work in you carry it through to completion.

The Authors

Part I

Getting Your Act Together

The Cast

The Bride and Groom

Uncle Joe and Aunt Maureen receive a Christmas card from their favorite niece, Melissa. As far as the new year is concerned, Melissa has only one thing on her mind. "The wedding is three months away," she writes. "Now the pressure is *really* on!"

Uncle Joe, the father of four boys, shakes his head and mutters, "Pressure? How much pressure can there be when the wedding is still three months away?" Aunt Maureen wisely keeps her thoughts to herself.

Do your parents have any extra closet or drawer space in their house? Of course not. We use up as much space as we have. The same with time. Your engagement, whatever its length, will be filled with details large and small. There are so many things to do and worry about that it often seems that there just isn't enough time or energy to prepare adequately for both a wedding and a marriage. However there are many aspects of putting together this biggest day of your life that prove to be good training for the 'Til Death Do Us Part marathon.

Setting Priorities

Once your love deepens to the point where you finally decide to form this lifelong mutual admiration society, you will begin to collect lists. It's unavoidable. They will come at you from a dizzying variety of sources: bridal magazines, etiquette books, the church, your mother, your partner, your partner's mother, your mother's partner, the photographer, the photographer's partner, and on and on and on.

All of these lists will start with either "should" or "must." This is because the author is convinced that what she or he is suggesting is more important than anything else that anyone else will suggest to you.

A single person has little trouble dealing with these demands of time and money. Acting alone it is easy to say yes or no and live with the decision. As half of a married couple you will have to consider the needs, resources and schedule of another person in making decisions that affect both of you.

A shrewd salesperson often calls on newlyweds, depending on the fact that each is unsure how the other really feels about the necessity of the product. Suddenly both partners are signing a contract for a big ticket item that neither wanted. When you were single, you would have told the salesperson immediately what he could do with all twenty-two volumes of Schwartz's World Encyclopedia. When you are married a few years, you will know whether your spouse considers it a worthwhile investment. But now it's a problem. During an engagement you have ample opportunity to exercise your aptitude for making joint decisions about all kinds of things, from the best place for a honeymoon to the size and location of an apartment. You will learn which decisions need consultation and which do not. It is more than likely that the groom will not care what kind of print is used on the invitations. But if the groom is a printer or a commercial artist, the wise bride learns that these things might be important to him. When the groom gets junk mail from every resort in the northern hemisphere, he should ask the bride whether she wants to see it before it goes into the circular file. During your engagement you will receive invitations from local businesses, civic organizations, and the adult friends of your parents. These invitations should not be accepted or refused by either of you until the other has been consulted.

Preparing for a wedding is a good time to have discussions that center on "This is important, or not important, for me. Now, what is important for us?"

Division of Labor

A visitor from Mars observing what goes on in planning
a modern American wedding would logically assume that
two women are getting married—one from twenty to thirty
years older than the other but similar in coloring and build.
In many weddings, the men are allowed to get away with
"Just tell me where you want me and when. I'll be there."

Brides who are willing to relieve grooms of all the picky
details involved in a wedding may find themselves forever
responsible for all the picky details involved in the
celebration of the major holidays as well as christenings,

graduations, birthdays, housewarmings and Super Bowl Sundays.

Brides who cheerfully write all the thank-you notes for both sides of the family will be expected to do Christmas cards every year just as cheerfully. The groom who shops for insurance or a mortgage all by himself teaches his partner nothing more useful than where to find the dotted line.

Maybe you enjoy talking to the photographer and the florist and the caterer, and your intended does not. Maybe you like doing income tax returns and your intended does not. If it seems more efficient to tackle these jobs alone, then maybe it is more efficient. But when you hear yourself muttering, "I sure could use some help around here," stop muttering and start communicating with your partner. If you have asked for help in the process, you will be able to rejoice together in the success of the product.

Compromise

Engaged couples quickly discover that "compromise" is a word married couples use when they really mean "giving in." Compromise is the foundation of those mythical 50-50 marriages. Has anyone ever known of a 50-50 relationship that lasted longer than twenty minutes? A 50-50 relationship is the one you have with a cab driver—you agree to pay the fare in return for a ride to your destination.

Compromise conjures images of two kids trading football cards—I'll give you a Neil Lomax and an Art Monk for your Walter Payton. Actually it's more like a birthday party. I'll give you what you need and want whether I get anything from you or not. This is expressed in the vows. Each of you promises to be true in good times and bad, to love and honor all the days of your life. Nowhere does the word "if" appear in the vows.

There are many situations in which a compromise is simply impossible. When the groom wants a brass ensemble to play at the wedding and the bride wants a jazz quartet, they will not be able to agree on a middle ground because there is none that will satisfy both negotiators. Later, when she wants a condo in Los Angeles and he wants a two-story Colonial in Baltimore, a rambler in Buzzard Lips, Wyoming will not be a compromise.

Engaged couples soon realize that compromise really means taking turns giving in cheerfully and gracefully. The challenge lies in making adjustments when one partner is giving in more often than the other. So when you hear yourselves arguing about whether to have the wedding at 11:00 or 11:30, don't end it with "Let's not fight about this." Go ahead and fight about it. It will be good practice for later on when one of you argues that Christmas just isn't Christmas without a real Christmas tree, and the other contends that an artificial one is cheaper and more practical. Or one insists that the children take piano lessons and the other always hated piano lessons. Or one wants to spend the income tax return on a computer and the other wants to remodel the bathroom. Decisions about career changes and family planning pale in comparison to the intensity and frequency of these other domestic discussions.

Amazing Social Graces

It's only a matter of time after the wedding when it will happen. The phone will ring, and the new bride will answer and be asked whether Mrs. Miniver is in. She will instruct the caller that a wrong number has been reached, give the interested party her mother-in-law's number and hang up. The new groom will attend the office party and introduce his lovely date as his wife, but somehow "wife" sounds funny when he says it out loud.

By the simple act of taking a spouse, you are entering a new segment of society. You will not look different and you may not feel different, but as married people you will be treated differently.

Throughout your teen years, your mother considered

you incapable of handling situations more complicated than operating a pay phone. Your father asked every spring if you remembered to get tags for your car. Whenever you acted half-human, your parents' friends would cluck appreciatively and murmur, "Such a nice boy." Now they will expect some very adult behavior to go along with your new lifestyle. The engagement period is a good time to sharpen some of the social skills your parents have tried to convince you were necessary, because now they are.

For instance, your parents are probably more than willing to help you plan the wedding, but they are just as busy during the day as you are. There is no reason that they should have to make phone calls, reservations and appointments for you.

Between now and the wedding, you will be showered often with gifts, invitations, compliments and advice. If you learn to be gracious in your acceptance and quick with your thanks while you are engaged, it will become second nature by the time you are married.

When you were single, you may have been slow to introduce yourself to others at social or business gatherings. When alone, a shy person may act invisible. But when your spouse is by your side, you may not consign her or him to the same fate. Whenever you encounter a friend or relative who does not know your partner, introductions are mandatory. A spouse who is not introduced promptly might understand that you are shy, that this is difficult for you and that you don't intend to cause hurt feelings. But you would do well to cultivate the thoughtful habit of demonstrating your love for your partner by proudly introducing him or her to all of your friends.

There are lots of interesting rules and helpful hints for developing all sorts of social skills. The etiquette book sitting right next to your Bible covers many other details besides who stands where in the receiving line. Read on. There are helpful guidelines for how to issue and respond to invitations, write thank-you notes, announce births, and correspond with the President (one never knows). Becoming familiar with correct procedures makes life easier, believe it or not, and frees you from worrying about the best way to go about being polite.

Formal announcement of your decision to marry engages you in any number of activities, some of which you may not have anticipated. Be attentive to these new demands and you'll get off to a great start.

Catholics Who Marry Other Christians or Non-Christians

Some years ago, it was presumed that Catholics only married Catholics. Any other arrangement was called a "mixed marriage" and was met with a considerable lack of enthusiasm. Progress has been made since the days when a Catholic marrying anyone other than another Catholic was given but two options: exchange vows in the priest's study, or live in sin.

It is not uncommon for two Christians of different denominations to enter marriage together. If the wedding is in a Catholic church, most priests are quite good about welcoming the participation of another minister. Some will invite the visitor to say a prayer, pronounce a blessing, read from Scripture or preach the homily. Much will depend on what is customary among local churches.

When a Catholic marries someone who is not Christian, the approach calls for both frankness and delicacy. Religious differences here are certainly more pronounced than between Lutherans and Catholics. To begin with, a Jew may certainly be understood not to want his or her marriage to a Catholic blessed "in the name of the Father, and of the Son, and of the Holy Spirit."

Many rabbis will not take part in a wedding uniting a Jew and Gentile. Before you call the caterer, call both the priest and rabbi, ask for an appointment, and see what the customs and traditions are in your area.

Some Bishops will permit a wedding of this sort to take place in a hotel ballroom or at another secular site; others will not. Ask your priest how this situation has been approached before. (See the Dispensation Form in Section II.)

Whenever he or she marries someone who isn t Catholic, the Catholic party is asked to promise that any children born of the marriage will be baptized and raised as Catholics. Some who prepare for marriage find this presents them with no problem; others have enormous difficulty with the idea. In any case, it is best that discussion on the matter begin immediately between bride and groom and all others concerned. Don't be shy about telling both priest and minister or rabbi that you want to talk it over with them. You won't be the first couple to ask; very few of the clergy were ordained yesterday. They have dealt with other couples who have had difficulties like your own before.

If one of you is being married in a church that is not your own, you should accompany your beloved to Sunday services there a few times before your wedding. The first time you experience the church filled with people should not be your wedding day. This simple suggestion is sure to lessen anxieties when the big day comes.

Whenever it begins to seem that there are just too many rules and guidelines, try to remember that the original intent of each rule or guideline is to protect your freedom and the continued existence of the group which gave you life.

Yes, yes, you're quite correct: it can be difficult. But if you need to struggle, remember that anything that doesn't kill you is bound to make you stronger!

Parents of the Bride and Groom

The parents of the bride and groom fulfilled their major obligation long ago by bringing you into the world and assisting you on the journey toward your mutual destiny. This sounds as though it ought to be enough, but there are a few loose ends to tie up as you separate from one family and begin another. Your parents' responsibilities on this most important of occasions do not vary from what they have been doing for most of your life.

The Mother of the Bride

The primary function of the bride's mother is to worry, or at least pretend to, while reassuring her daughter that there is absolutely nothing to worry about—where the wedding is concerned. Where the marriage is concerned, she is responsible for reminding the bride at least once a week (daily during the week before the wedding) that it isn't too late to back out. She is not talking about parallel parking.

The mother of the bride is allowed to blow up once a day over milk being left out or the post office being closed for Leif Ericson's birthday. For months she will have to act civil to strangers who infuriate her. Thus, the caterer gets, "Oh, no, Mr. Davenport, we understand that the icing will have to be vanilla instead of almond," which is why her beloved family members get, "Why the hell can't people around here *rinse* their *dishes* before they put them in the *dishwasher?*"

The Father of the Bride

While his wife should not shed tears in public until their daughter walks down the aisle (at which time it is

mandatory), the father of the bride may weep while sorting through family pictures or watching Hallmark commercials.

When paying the bills, the father of the bride should be heard to sigh and comment on the low cost of aluminum extension ladders, promising to invest in one for his other daughters.

The father of the bride must be in the house or immediately available at all times on the day of the wedding Yes, he will be in the way. Yes, his wife would probably do better without his help. But heaven help him if he should suggest that he could easily get in nine holes of golf before the wedding, even if it's true. He will never live it down. By the time the story reaches its tenth anniversary, everyone will laugh about how Bill took off to Palm Springs for a golf tournament and made it back barely in time to walk down the aisle.

The Mother of the Groom

It has been suggested that the job of the groom's mother is to wear beige and shut up. Usually she is more than willing to do this unless shared financial responsibility dictates shared decision making. Recognizing that discretion is the far better part of valor, the groom's mother prefers to keep her opinions to herself and save them for her own daughter's wedding.

The Father of the Groom

Curiously, no one can quite figure out exactly what the groom's father does. His role seems to be limited to mingling at the reception, while pretending to know people he's never seen before. To this end he is advised to practice his best back slap and the following lines: "Has there been enough weather for you?" "Yes, she *is* lovely. We're very pleased." "I seem to have misplaced my wife."

When the parents of the bride or the groom do not find themselves married to one another on a day that beats them senseless with the sanctity of marriage, they must be happy for their children. After all it is their day, as they have so often said during the past year. As they enter yet another important stage of adulthood, they have every right to expect their elders to conduct themselves with dignity and maturity. And parents have every right to enjoy themselves and the company of their friends and relatives on this exciting day.

The Priest

Even though you minister the sacrament of matrimony to one another, the Church requires the presence of one of its ordained ministers, a bishop, priest, or deacon, to witness your vows.

In approaching the priest, assume that he is still around because he wants to be helpful. Priests are usually nice guys and can be counted on to assist in planning this most important liturgy. They respond well in situations where they are called on as helpers and not as adversaries.

Ask any priest in the world when he gets his first clue that someone is too young or simply not ready for marriage. The universal answer: when mom calls to reserve the church and set up an interview. O.K., O.K., if you are in Tokyo and your beloved is in Kansas and you're coming home to Oregon for the wedding, we have a different case entirely. But the current thinking on the matter is that if you are old enough to get married, you are old enough to call a priest.

Actually, the first contact should not be on the phone but in person after Mass. The priest will be the guy standing by the door greeting worshipers. Just grab his hand, pump it up and down like everyone else, and introduce yourself if he does not know you. On another Sunday, reintroduce yourself and say, "I would like to call you and talk about a wedding date. When is the best time to reach you?" Don't try to make the appointment on Sunday. He has too many things going on and probably does not have a datebook concealed under his vestments.

When you do reach Father Przybocki on the phone, after learning how to pronounce his name correctly, mention that you have introduced yourself on previous Sundays and which Mass you attend (you have been attending, haven't you, and not just dashing in at 10:45 to catch Father P. after

10:00 Mass?). Then tell him that you would like to make an appointment to meet and find out what is necessary to arrange a wedding at St. Eudora's of the Burning Bush.

If you are not currently worshiping as a Catholic, you may have some difficulty securing the services of a priest (and why do you want to anyway?). Catholic people have a right to the sacraments, but there seems to be no fail-safe way of proving that you are a Catholic other than celebrating the Eucharist regularly. Reciting the Apostles' Creed from memory while clutching a glow-in-the-dark rosary just doesn't cut it. If you have slipped in your practice, you can go home again, Thomas Wolfe to the contrary. Start worshiping regularly and you can be sure that all you need will be available to you.

Perhaps you have a priest friend or relative who you would like to officiate. Most priests will be only too glad to have Father Frankie, who took the bride to the senior prom and is now ordained, come and do the honors. (If Father Frankie entered the seminary right after the bride broke off her engagement to him, it might be difficult for him to witness her marriage to someone else.) Remember, in all instances, to ask the pastor rather than inform. Few priests object to having others officiate in their parishes, but you won't know until you've asked.

The Best Man

The best man attends the groom and sees that all happens as smoothly as possible.

The best man begins work at the rehearsal, helping to round up the strays so that events can begin at the appointed hour.

The events preceding the wedding are often the most festive. The best man shepherds the groom throughout these festivities and makes sure that there is always a driver who has refrained from alcohol and any other debilitating substances; he sees that the one with the car keys in his pocket has 7-Up in his glass.

Should anyone decide that it would be fun to help the groom to drink to excess or engage in any questionable activity that might prevent his alert attendance where and when he is expected, it is the best man's job to say no. The groom must never be put in an impossible situation. It is the best man's job to get there first and see to it that such decisions need not be made by the one about to commit himself to marriage. The best man runs interference in any situation which may hamper the groom's ability to function on the wedding day.

The best man is usually the keeper of the rings, bringing them to the ceremony and keeping them in his pocket until they are needed. He is not advised to put them both on his own fingers; they are too easily stuck there or may be lost if they fit him too loosely.

Some few best men need to hear the caution that they should take the rings out of the jeweler's box before putting them into their pockets!

It is usually the best man's task to give the priest the offering which he has been given earlier, usually by the groom. This should be done privately and discreetly. The

check or cash should be in an envelope or card and never palmed off in a handclasp as one might to a bellhop who leads the happy couple to the honeymoon suite.

In most states, the signature of the best man is required with that of the maid of honor and the priest on the wedding license. The best man gets the license from the bride or groom before the rehearsal, asks the priest when he would like to be given the license, and presents it at the appointed time.

It is not the best man's job to paint rude or vulgar sayings in shaving cream on the bridal car. Those who feel so inspired should turn immediately to the essay for the ushers.

The Maid or Matron of Honor

Like those of the best man, the tasks of the maid or matron of honor are few but significant.

She attends the bride and sees that all happens smoothly and sensibly. Anything that might fluster the bride at this happy hour is dealt with politely and with as little fuss as possible.

The festive events preceding the wedding call for her very special attention. She ensures that there is a driver when needed who is straight and sober and can be counted on safely to deliver those who will not be both partying and driving.

While the best man looks after the rings, the maid of honor looks after the bridal bouquet when the bride can't hold it because, for example, she is holding the groom's hand while reciting her vows. This attendant also sees that the train of the bridal gown, whenever the bride has moved to a new position, is arranged the way both the designer and God had in mind.

She joins with the best man, at least in most states, in signing the marriage license as proof positive that what you have seen exchanged, the consent and vows, is now the law.

Bridesmaids and Groomsmen

Who needs to be there in order for you to get yourselves legally married? The two of you are the ministers of the sacrament. You're needed. The priest is necessary as the Church's witness and as the state's functionary as well. Also needed are two more witnesses, usually the maid or matron of honor and the best man.

The liturgical function of these last two is small: they stand where they are told to stand, they witness the event and, in most states, they affix their signatures to the marriage license.

As small as their function is, it is major in comparison to that of the bridesmaids and groomsmen. Outside of attending parties, wearing the appointed clothes, and having a place in the procession, these folks seem not to have a function which differs from the rest of the assembly.

There is nothing for attendants to sign other than the guest book. However, with the rest of the congregation, they join enthusiastically in prayer and song as they witness the marriage event.

On this day many brides and grooms enjoy being surrounded by their families and friends who are dressed as members of the wedding party.

There seems to be no rule about the number of those you can include as long as you realize that their function is merely decorative or supportive. Care should be taken not to exclude siblings who may be hurt when left out but who might be too shy to request that they be included. Those who cannot afford the expense should not be shy about asking to have a place as an honored guest rather than as a member of the wedding party.

Some of the attendants may be asked to give assistance to the ushers in getting the church ready and the congregation seated. In some places, the title groomsmen is not used: there are only bridesmaids and ushers.

There seems to be at least one story in the national press each year recounting a wedding which has just been entered in the Guinness Book of World Records for having included the greatest number of attendants. Perhaps one day there will be a wedding where every person in the church is in a tux or bridesmaid's dress. You, however, may wish to spend some time considering the real significance of the wedding event and the part truly played by friends and family. Invite them to be in the wedding party in numbers you consider to be in keeping with the sacramental nature of the event.

The Crew

Musicians

The musicians you ask to assist you in making worship ought to be folks who have made music in church before. It is very difficult to take a perfectly fine piano player and singer from your favorite bar and transplant them into your designated church. Their fit is not always perfect. The ministry of music is not entertainment, and folks perfectly comfortable in one field cannot always easily translate into the other.

You are safest and less likely to be surprised by error or oversight if you hire the musicians who usually work in your parish or who come with the recommendation of the priest who, you will remember, attends more weddings in a season than most folks do in two-thirds of a lifetime.

Most couples ask an organist to provide their music. This need not be your only choice. Any number of instruments can serve the Church at prayer. If you want a piano, harp, strings or brass in addition to or instead of the organ, make the necessary arrangements with your priest and the musicians as far in advance as possible.

Ask the musicians their fee and pay them at or before the rehearsal.

The Reader

Aunt Lulu is serving punch; little cousin Edwin is watching over the guest book; second-cousin-once-removed Eunice is personal attendant to the bride and Uncle Phil will bartend while Aunt Gert parks cars.

We only need something for brother-in-law George to do. And the only job left is reading the Scriptures during the ceremony. We'll have to ask him, right?

Wrong.

For several reasons.

If George hasn't proclaimed the Scriptures publicly before, asking him to solo for the first time when all the rellies are gathered is unfair. Even if he did once have the lead in the senior high play, reading in church is a different type of affair. First, it's a ministry. Second, it requires training. Third, not all persons are disposed to or comfortable with the task.

George may not want to say no because he wants to help and be part of the festivity. On the other hand, if he doesn't do well, his embarrassment and your disappointment will not lessen tensions on what is usually a difficult enough day anyway.

If you don't have a family member or friend who has proclaimed Scriptures for the assembly before, the wedding day is not the proper time to start. Tell the priest if you are having difficulty locating a reader and he will give you the guidance or assistance you need in recruiting the proper person.

Before you invite anyone to read at your wedding, ask the priest what particular guidelines apply at your parish. Asking in advance will make your life much easier.

One reader may be selected for the Old Testament reading and another to proclaim the New Testament reading. Or one reader may do both. In the Catholic tradition, reading the Gospel before the assembly is a task reserved for the ordained.

The reader should be reconciled to the translation of the Scripture provided for use in the church. He or she should not ad lib a new translation. This too often results in mismatched verbs and nouns and a missed sense of what the scriptural author intended.

Here's an important point: there are many different translations of the Scriptures, so don't ask the reader to practice from his or her own Bible. Make a copy of the readings you select from the back of this book; the translation found here is the same one found in the lectionary used in all Catholic churches. Stick with this book and avoid any confusion! It should be noted, too, that the readings should be proclaimed at the wedding from a handsome, hardcover book, not a paperback, to emphasize the solemn nature of what the assembly is about.

It should be determined whether or not book and reader will be in the entrance procession.

The reader should check the spot where he or she is to sit, with the congregation or in the sanctuary, and should try out the public address system before, during or after the rehearsal.

The priest will give a cue when the reading is to begin at the wedding. Those who are nervous about being ready at the appropriate moment should ask what the cue will be.

Remember that to proclaim the Scriptures for the Christian assembly is an honor that should not be taken lightly.

We haven't solved your problem about George. Sorry.

Ushers

Some think that ushers are groomsmen who didn't make the final cut, friends who are honored by having some small part in the wedding ceremony.

That is not our Catholic view. We look on ushers as free labor for eight hours.

The ushers' tasks are many and varied. Much responsibility is placed on them. The ushers have more opportunity to make mistakes that will influence the flow of the ceremony than almost any other player.

The ushers' duties begin at the rehearsal where they find and learn how to operate the phones and to locate the trash cans and bathrooms which will be needed later. They listen attentively to the priest's instructions and ask for clarification when it may not be clear what is expected of them.

On the wedding day, the ushers' duties begin well before the ceremony. They are to be at the church, unless an individual parish policy differs, no less than forty-five minutes before the ceremony is to begin. It is not the job of the priest to tie bow ties for ushers who haven't worn them before; when they arrive, they should already be dressed.

They are to make sure that the priest has help in moving any sanctuary furniture that is to be moved. Also, they see that the white aisle runner, if it is to be used, is placed securely at the head of the aisle. It is fastened down so it can be unrolled. The string for unrolling the runner is placed where it can be easily grabbed when needed and must be long enough so that a six foot usher need not walk down the aisle stooped over in imitation of the hunchback of Notre Dame.

Some guests will insist on arriving ahead of the ushers and sitting in the back pew, aisle seat. If the ushers allow guests to sit wherever they choose, and the 170 guests are scattered across a church that seats 900, the bride will enter, think that no one has come to her wedding, be upset, and it will be the ushers' fault.

Better to plan for no disappointments. Early arrivers who sit in the back should be invited forward: "Friend, come higher! It's a large church; you'll see and hear better closer up. Will you follow me, please?"

The usher extends his arm, the lady takes his arm, the gentleman follows, and the guests are brought forward. The usher places his hand on the pew the guests are to enter, steps to one side and, after they are seated, returns to the vestibule to greet the next comers.

If the usher is a woman, she does not extend her arm to those she seats, but walks by the side of the female guest and the man follows. The procedure is then the same as outlined above.

Ushers shouldn't ask "Friend of the bride or the groom?" but should presume that all are friends of both and should divide the guests evenly between sides unless a specific request is made.

Some guests will insist that there are bride's and groom's sides in a church. The usher's job is to humor them. Which side is which? To answer this question, God has given statues to his Church. In traditional Catholic churches, there is often a statue of Mary on the left as one enters. She defines the bride's side. A statue of Joseph (or the Sacred Heart) is often on the right. He marks the gentleman's side.

After the aisle seats are filled with the early arriving guests who want a good view, those next to arrive are seated by the side aisles.

When all the guests are seated, the grandparents are ushered in—first the paternal and then maternal grandparents of the groom, then of the bride. If parents are not in the procession, the mother of the groom is then escorted to her seat, followed by her husband. Last to enter before the games begin is the mother of the bride on the arm of the usher of her choice.

Seating arrangements for families diversified through remarriage should be planned before the rehearsal and directions given to the ushers.

The carpet is then rolled down the aisle. Don't leave the cardboard tube found in the center of the runner at the back of the church where it will be tripped over. If the ushers have attended properly to their duties, it is now only fifteen seconds before the ceremony begins and their tasks are not yet complete.

Any guests who have not yet been seated are late. They are asked politely to remain in the back until all in the procession have made their way into the sanctuary. The late-comers are then seated, but only by the side aisles.

The ushers may not desert the church during the ceremony to go out and paint vulgar sayings on the car with shaving cream. This practice not only is harmful to the paint and offensive to many of those involved (is "Hot Springs Tonight" really a travel destination you think needs to be mentioned on the car?), but it also gets in the way of duties inside.

Should there be any difficulty during the ceremony, the priest may need to call on the ushers for help. If it is warm and windows need to get themselves opened, for example. Or if someone faints. Or if a guest with a beeper is paged and needs to find the phone which the usher, aware of his duties, located the night before at the rehearsal. Or if the runner wrinkles and needs to be straightened. Also, some women in high heels sometimes have a difficult time walking on the plastic or paper runners and need assistance in the Communion line or leaving the church.

In short, the ushers are a very significant presence and are needed far more in the church than they are in the parking lot.

Their tasks are not over when the ceremony is over. They have asked where the runner is to be stored or disposed of. They assist in moving plants or furniture as needed. Should anyone have involved himself or herself in the pagan custom of throwing rice, the ushers seek out brooms to clear away the mess so that those attending the next function in the church need not risk a fall by walking over the debris.

This having been done, the ushers brush themselves and each other off and proceed with all appropriate haste to the subsequent festivities.

Junior Members of the Party

Who is old enough to walk down the aisle ahead of you on your wedding day?

That depends. Life is not without risks, exciting and otherwise. A wedding during which everything proceeds as perfectly as planned leaves no legacy of amusing family stories that become delightfully embellished over the years.

However, professional wedding goers can tell plenty of wedding stories that are not so amusing. These usually feature people who are inexperienced, unprepared or not quite sure what is expected of them when the curtain goes up. Flower girls and ring bearers often find themselves in this awkward position.

More than one father of the bride has had to escort his daughter down the aisle while carrying a howling child who decided that this game wasn't much fun and she didn't want to play after all. We who are older tend to forget the terrors that children suffer.

Maybe you are ambivalent about the idea of dressing little ones like grown-ups and expecting them to conduct themselves like grown-ups. But your Aunt Lucy, who is extremely unambivalent about everything, is certain that your twin cousins would look darling as flower girl and ring bearer. If it is a risk worth taking for the sake of family peace or your own pleasure, launch little Fred and Ethel after the other attendants have made their way down the aisle, but before the maid of honor. That way, if the children balk, the maid of honor can gently take their hands and guide them to their appointed places. Aunt Lucy should sit up front next to the center aisle so the children can see her, head straight for her pew and sit quietly by her side for the duration.

Perhaps you pale at the possibility of having to listen to six verses of what used to be your favorite hymn while your niece empties her flower basket petal by petal, returning for more when she runs out. Suggest to Aunt Lucy that you wouldn't dream of putting her and Uncle Ricky through the time and expense involved in such an endeavor. You might also suggest that Fred and Ethel dress up and assist the ushers in handing out programs, with Aunt Lucy close by. The children will not be disappointed if the importance of their job is impressed upon them.

Does this fail to answer your very simple question about who is old enough to walk down the aisle ahead of you on your wedding day? Here is a rule of thumb: using anyone under the age of $5^1/_2$ (the half in this case is significant) is risky. But perhaps you would rather rule with your heart than your thumb. Some couples take more of a chance with their thirty year old best man than they do with their three year old ring bearer.

Altar Servers

Many churches use altar servers for weddings only when the bride and/or groom have family members or friends they would like to honor by asking their service for the special day.

Some priests feel they can get along well enough without servers. Others provide their own as a way for grade schoolers either to be of service or to earn $5.

Ask your priest what the custom is at your church. If you want to bring your own servers, you usually may.

But what if the servers are girls?

This custom is accepted in some places while it is unheard of or forbidden elsewhere.

Before you make plans with cousins Angela and Angelo to come all the way from Proctor to be servers in their native garb, you had better first check the local custom.

The Photographer

A visual record of your wedding is sure to be pleasing to you in years to come. A good photographer will help you preserve these memories.

As soon as you have decided on a wedding date and secured the church, select and book your photographer. If you don't get to him or her soon enough, you may be disappointed to find out that the photographer is scheduled farther in advance than you had imagined to be necessary.

Keep in mind that your wedding is a religious event and that the activities surrounding that event are to be in keeping with both the dignity of the sacrament and the place in which it is celebrated.

The church is not a studio. No altar furniture should be moved. Plan your photographs to capture your special faces and clothing and distinguishing features of the house of the Church in which your wedding takes place.

Most parishes have firm rules about how much time is permitted before and after the wedding for photography. Be aware that these guidelines are for your benefit; no one wants to allow a photographer to begin taking pictures at noon for a 7 P.M. wedding. Remember that the photographer works for you and not the other way around. Guidelines are intended to prevent such suggestions from becoming reality. Remember, too, that pastors and church employees are no strangers to weddings and they know how much time is or should be taken for photographs.

Many couples have found that taking pictures before the wedding helps to relax them and allows them to get more quickly to the reception after the ceremony so that guests are not kept waiting.

Say "Pumpkin cheesecake!" as you flash those ivories.

How Much To Give Whom for Doing What

Since the celebration of your union as husband and wife inspires thoughts of love and romance and never-ending bliss, it is difficult to determine how much to pay people for their priceless services. Don't let that difficulty stop you from doing it.

Assume that it will cost to use the church even though your parents are major stockholders and faithfully spend every Saturday at church cooking, cleaning and painting whatever needs to be cooked, cleaned, and painted. Ask the priest or someone in the parish office about the standard fee. If none is specified, don't think you are off the hook when asked to make an appropriate gift.

Before you write the check for the church, consider first: the cost of your reception, the price tag of the honeymoon, the rent for the first month in your new apartment. Ask yourself if your wedding liturgy is any less important.

The following suggestions will help you with this decision.

Do you wish to be modest? Take the cost of the groom's outfit and add it to the cost of the cake. Divide by two. This amount would be modest compensation for the time, energy and resources used to get you up to the altar.

Want to be a bit more generous? Take the cost of the bride's clothing. Add to it the cost of the wedding photography. Divide by two. This amount would be a more generous gift and probably a more accurate reflection of the value of services rendered on your behalf.

If you are still unsure, consult with the priest. Though you may find it awkward to talk about money, be assured that he overcame his inhibitions about it long ago. A word to the wise groom (who traditionally provides the offering):

Don't ask the priest "How much does it cost?" because he may well ask you "How much is she worth?"

In some areas, the gift you make goes directly to the parish. In some areas it is considered a gift to the priest. If this makes a difference to you, please ask how the matter is handled in your area. When considering what size gift to make for services rendered and buildings used, remember that weddings are expensive affairs.

It is the best man's task to give the priest the offering from the bride and groom. This should be done privately and discreetly. The check or cash should be in a card enclosed in an envelope and never palmed off as one might for a solicitous bellhop or maitre d'.

The musicians, photographer, caterer, and other local entrepreneurs will tell you up front what financial reimbursement they expect in return for helping create all this magic. When you call upon friends to perform these tasks, things get a little trickier but not much. If they are professionals, find out how much they customarily receive and offer to pay it. Please remember that close friends and family members may not wish to work on your wedding day

If your brother is arranging the flowers, your roommate is singing and your uncle is witnessing your vows, thoughtful gifts are appropriate. It is customary to buy gifts for every member of your wedding party including the flower girl and ring bearer. Ask the priest about the standard tip for the altar servers, but if five bucks apiece doesn't do it, they are too old for the job.

Prompt thank-you notes are called for all around—for both moms and dads, friends who helped in any way and your priest who spent Friday night and most of Saturday and Sunday in church. If you are starting to turn chartreuse at the mere thought of one more thank-you note, perhaps one of you is shouldering too much of this important responsibility. Tackle them together. Isn't that the very reason you decided to wed?

The Costumes

Wedding Clothes

Wedding day is dress-up day. It is a time to look and feel your very best.

The color for men who want to dress formally is black. Magenta, white, aqua, and peach tuxes and cummerbunds are formal clothes that beg to be left in the showroom. Take a long hard look at those ruffles, flourishes and pastels. Do they draw attention away from your Mel Gibson bone structure and your Tom Selleck smile? Do they compete with the clean graceful lines of the bride's gown? Will the congregation assume that you are the lead guitarist for Little Archie and the Innuendos scheduled to perform at the reception?

If you are the lead guitarist for Little Archie and the Innuendos, and are accustomed to wearing a tux to work, by all means wear that tux to your wedding. It would fit well and suggest that this is how you are accustomed to dress and are not disguised for the evening as a member of European royalty. If you are not a musician or a member of European royalty, consider wedding clothes that are more a part of your life. The alternative is simple and attractive enough to be considered revolutionary.

Slacks and a blazer.

"Slacks and a blazer? Are you kidding? Where can we rent slacks and blazers?"

Don't rent. Buy.

"Buy? You mean tell all the guys in my wedding party to *buy* clothes for the occasion?"

Why not? Women have done it for years. Besides, a fair number of the men will already own a navy blue blazer and a nice pair of grey or khaki slacks. If they don't, they should. Your mothers insist on more formality? Buy pinstripe or charcoal grey suits. A red silk tie would be a fine present from the groom and all men in the party could look well put together and handsome in clothes that can be purchased for little more than the cost of rented ones. Your friends will appreciate being able to make a smooth transition from your wedding to a hot date or a job interview.

"But they might not match!"

Only the Marine Corps marching band and the Rockettes need to match. Khaki is khaki and, anyway, all eyes will be on the bride.

Be cautious with rented clothing; the more your physique deviates from 5'9¾" and 147 pounds, the less chance you have for a perfect fit. Real clothes can be purchased and altered well in advance of the wedding

wherever the purchaser happens to live. You want to see a circus? Just wait until seven men from across the country converge on the Duds for Studs Tux Emporium in your home town three days before the wedding. You will be faced with sleeves that are too short, inseams that are too long, hems that are too obvious and not enough time or energy to do anything about it.

If the men can be so practical, what about the women?

The bride is allowed to shell out a ridiculous sum of money for a dress that she will wear only once. Her attendants should not have to follow suit since they may very well find themselves traipsing down the aisle for more than one bride. Why impose a financial hardship on your friends for the sake of a prom dress that will turn into a closet ornament the day after the wedding?

How about midlength skirts, in a seasonal fabric, with silk blouses and bows? This would be elegant, classy, comfortable and a sure crowd pleaser. And the bride needn't blush when she assures her friends that they can wear these outfits again.

Where flower girls are concerned, a truly considerate bride will not ask her four year old niece to spend close to twelve hours in a dry-clean-only gown that is destined to become undone, torn or covered with lobster Newburg by the end of the day. A short fancy dress with ruffles, a pinafore, white tights and patent leather shoes will make her and everyone else more comfortable. Ribbons and bows that fit the color scheme can be added.

Plan to exercise good taste and sound judgment as you select the wardrobe for this most special day. Your wedding may be more memorable, and more imitated, than even you had thought possible.

Setting the Stage

Whose Wedding Is This Anyway?

Once you and your beloved announce your intentions you will hear as many opinions about the wedding ceremony as you ask for and then some.

There are two prevailing philosophies about weddings.

First, there are those loving friends and relatives who peer through a lens that makes life larger than itself. Their theory is that your wedding day exists to make all your dreams come true in a lavish ceremony guaranteed to send Cinderella back to the drawing board. After all, you only get married once, the saying goes (despite statistics to the contrary), and you might as well do it right. Right has come to mean cramming more guests, music, flowers, liquor, food, and confusion into one day than is currently allowed by law in most states. With this philosophy, financial resources dwindle as the guest list expands.

Other friends tend to be more far-sighted. They see your wedding day as only one day out of an entire lifetime together, and the simpler the better. Two thousand dollars for a dress that she'll wear once? Wouldn't they rather spend the money on a nice side by side frost-free refrigerator freezer? You will hear about Aunt Rita who was married in the rectory wearing her WAC uniform and carrying a handful of nasturtiums from Grandma's garden, and it was a *lovely* ceremony, and she and Uncle Jack have been happily married for over forty years now. (Of course when you talk to Aunt Rita, she might slip you a generous check and advise you to do it right.)

The Do It Right people see your wedding as a family celebration, an excellent excuse for people to get together for a great party. Expensive but well worth it.

The Hold Your Horses people see weddings as a

voracious beast requiring financial nourishment as each new detail is added.

Occasionally you might hear this attitude expressed by your priest. Year after year as he witnesses a seemingly endless parade of clothing, flowers, and trimmings, he wonders how struggling families can justify the expense. On the other hand, when it comes to holy orders, you'll find very few men willing to slip over to the chancery and be ordained on the floor in front of the bishop's desk.

The easiest wedding (if there is such a thing as an easy wedding) involves people with similar ideas. It happens.

However when you find yourselves screaming "But it's

our wedding!" it's time to examine your feelings about the wedding day.

Weddings are meant to be one to a customer and as such should be custom-made with both families in mind.

Yes, you are the ones getting married. But as adults you realize that other people's plans and dreams must also be considered. It is a sad bride who after five years still pouts because she didn't get the priest she wanted. Or the flowers arrived with lavender ribbons instead of lilac. Or her best friend was too pregnant to be her matron of honor.

You have already shared many special days together and have many more to look forward to. Your wedding day will not be the first, last, or only important day in your life together as a couple.

It is only once in a lifetime, so work hard and have fun making it as lovely as possible. At the same time, take steps to ensure that your marriage will be just as special and full of love and joy as your wedding.

Choosing a Church

Even should you be successful in finding a priest who thinks it would be both fun for him and meaningful for you to be married while skydiving over Central Park, it is unlikely that you'll find a bishop who will permit it.

Most insist that weddings take place in a parish church or chapel, and not in a hotel ballroom or even in your parents' living room.

Before you take up the familiar battle cry "But it's *our* wedding!" remember that the sacrament of matrimony is a public commitment involving more than just those immediately and intimately involved.

As a sacrament, your marriage is a visible and tangible sign to all the world of God's love. You are the light of the world, reflecting God's love for all to see. Therefore the ceremony must be highly visible and not hidden under a bushel basket.

Your love is enshrined and your commitment is made within a Catholic liturgy. Even though it is your wedding, and all gathered pray for and with you, it is the Church's liturgy. And because, in theory, all liturgy is open to the Catholic public (don't tell this to the Kennedys), the Church's ceremony takes place in the Church's house.

These are the reasons that your priest will probably not agree to meet you on the beach, at the park, in a hot air balloon or anywhere other than a church or chapel that has been designated as a place for the celebration of the wedding liturgy.

Most weddings take place in the bride's church. Certainly there are other possibilities, but if you embark on a shopping expedition for a church with more parking or prettier windows, you may encounter a pastor who is less than sympathetic to your wishes.

Many parishes cannot accommodate wedding parties for those who are not members of that particular parish. If the parking lot and the windows are that important to you, join the parish (and don't be astonished when you receive envelopes and a request to serve on the parish council). Churches are built to serve the needs of the faithful community. If you have no intention of belonging to and worshiping with that community, chances are slim that you will be married there. If the parish was yours as a child and your parents are still there, tell the priest because he may not remember you even if he knows your parents.

Some parishes require a deposit to reserve your wedding date. This deposit is refunded if everything is in working order when the wedding is over, or is applied to the fee stipulated for use of the church.

When you contract the use of the church, you will agree to the terms set by the parish office or liturgy commission. Usually these are not arbitrary rules written by a crabby priest for his own convenience. They are policies drawn up by those who regularly work in and worship in these buildings. It's wise to get the guidelines in writing before you plan to paint the pews to match the bridesmaids' gowns or install Dolby quadraphonic speakers behind the altar or videotape the ceremony.

Some rules reinforce your own common sense regarding the behavior of the wedding party and your guests. Though you often enjoy the company of guests who eat, drink and smoke in your house, you can understand why these activities are not permitted in a church. It is your responsibility to communicate these and other restrictions to the wedding party before the rehearsal. Other stipulations might address the use of tape on the pews, arrangement of sanctuary furniture, placement of candles and banners, which rooms are designated for use by the wedding party, how early you may arrive and how long you may stay.

The rules governing the use of the church hall, if that is where you plan to hold the reception, are different in content but similar in philosophy to those governing use of the church. Your friends, who are now your guests rather than fellow worshipers, are encouraged to eat, drink and be as merry as possible within the bounds of good taste and the boundaries of the social hall. But you can understand that the church hall should not resemble the scene of an all-night bacchanal when the pre-schoolers toddle in for Sunday school the next morning.

Most couples do not intentionally inconvenience the parishioners who will use the worship space when they are done with it. But it is so easy to get caught up in the excitement of the day and forget how things looked when you were still single. Written guidelines help you remember how to put things back in order.

If the pastor has a right to expect proper and safe use of the facilities, you have a right to expect some assistance in adhering to these rules. Trash receptacles should be accessible and empty. You should know where and when to obtain keys to the rooms you will need and where and when to return them. The restrooms should be stocked with necessary supplies. And you should have the phone number of someone who can answer your questions patiently and completely.

Flowers, Candles and Aisle Runners

Pick a man. Any man. Or choose a woman, but not one who has been attending weddings with an eye toward planning one of her own. Now ask this person to describe the flowers at the last wedding he or she attended.

If that last wedding played itself out in the shade of an ostentatious display of greens and cut flowers, or if the only vegetation was a single, naked carnation peeking out from the neck of a Coke bottle, chances are that your question will be answered quickly and to the accompaniment of a thigh being slapped. Most people, however, cannot answer the question.

The moral is: flowers and plants can enhance the atmosphere when you exchange your vows. They are not central to the action; rather they are intended to complement it. Buy, rent, or borrow accordingly.

Consider what is easily available to you seasonally. Winter brides in Minnesota have taken baskets and filled them with pine boughs, while in Arizona cactuses can be trimmed with Christmas ornaments.

Some florists will rent Boston ferns, or you can buy them and give them as gifts to particularly helpful family members when the ceremony is over. If you keep one for your own apartment, don't interpret it as a bad omen if the poor thing dies shortly after your honeymoon. Ferns seem to be more delicate than most marriages.

Looking for something borrowed, one bride used the hanging fuschia baskets from her mother's front porch and intercepted geraniums slated to be planted in the garden. They looked quite festive in the sanctuary; even the men noticed them.

Many churches do not permit artificial flowers of any kind. If your uncle is a silk flower broker and you had your

heart set on the discount, please consult with your pastor or
local liturgy committee before making any decisions. You
might also ask yourself, if not your uncle, whether part of
the charm of flowers is that they don't last forever.

Ask your pastor or those who assist in your church
which arrangements have been the most memorable.
Chances are that those most clearly remembered had a
personal touch and were not lavish or outrageously
expensive.

Candles and aisle runners may also be used to add a bit
of pomp to your circumstances. Aisle runners were first
employed in churches where floors were dirtier and colder
than those of our modern churches. Though this is rarely a

problem today, some families like the look of rolling out the white carpet for the bridal party.

Processing down an aisle covered with plastic is as elegant as sitting on a couch treated the same way. On carpeted floors, a plastic runner becomes almost lethal as it is punctured by high heels. On any floor, it crinkles, wrinkles, and does not seem to know what to do with itself when the liturgy is over. Guests may kick it out of the way as they leave the church, or some helpful soul may gather it up and shove it into a corner in the vestibule before the ushers can dispose of it properly.

Linen aisle runners can be rented from your florist or a local linen supply firm. No need to measure the length of the aisle. Your supplier should have the vital statistics on every church in town.

Candles, like children, are lovely to have around until they start leaving lasting evidence of their presence. If you want to use rented candelabra, your pastor might insist that the floor under them be protected. More plastic. The candles already in place in the sanctuary give off the same soft glow and are approved for neatness. If you provide your own candles for parish-owned fixtures, make sure that they are made to last as long as the liturgy.

Fire codes and pastoral preferences might dictate the number and placement of your candles. Know your limits before you make detailed plans.

The Procession

Getting from point B to point A is a simple matter unless point B is the back of the church, point A is the altar, and three hundred misty eyes are following your every move.

Because of the importance and festivity of the occasion, you will want to process in some fashion. The Late-For-Mass-Side-Aisle-Shuffle will not do.

Here are some of your options:

The standard lineup is for the bride to be preceded by her attendants and escorted by her father, stepfather, oldest brother or whoever happens to be the highest ranking male in the family (figuring *that* out is up to you). Some might say that this is a sign that the bride is being given away. Nonsense. Catholic theology and Catholic liturgy make it clear that the man and the woman both enter marriage freely and of their own desire.

The male attendants walk with their partners or wait, with the groom, near the sanctuary for the women, and escort them to their appointed positions.

The bride and the groom may want to walk together preceded by their parents and matched pairs of attendants. This configuration neatly settles any squabbles about who will escort the bride to the sanctuary, but approach this innovation delicately. The bride and groom have the years ahead to walk side by side. For the father of the bride, this is a rare chance to get all dressed up and stand proudly next to the woman he still thinks of as his little girl. The bride who wishes to deviate slightly from tradition might approach her mother first.

Some grooms come in procession with their parents, three abreast, and wait near the sanctuary for the bride escorted by her parents. Should you decide to do it this way, it is best to avoid the linebacker lunge. Do not hook arms as a threesome and charge forward. The groom offers his arm to his mother and either holds his father's hand (practice this first—you probably have not done it since first grade!) or walks with dad by his side.

The bride who comes down the aisle with both parents puts one arm through her father's and holds her bouquet in that hand. She then holds her mother's hand and walks with dignity down the aisle.

If you have doubts, try out different approaches at home. This can be a lot of fun with the junior members of the family humming "Here Comes the Bride" off-key and the bride holding a medium-sized bowling trophy to simulate her bouquet. After you decide how you would like to process, check it out with the priest when you meet to plan the liturgy, then write it down, in stone, with the signatures of two sober witnesses. At the rehearsal you may not change your mind. This is for your own protection. If you seem to waver, everyone from the soloist to the best man's mother-in-law will have an opinion and you'll be there for hours rehearsing options before returning to your original idea.

An important distinction to remember is that the parade that begins your wedding is really a liturgical procession. If you want to win points with the priest, ask him whether he thinks that this procession should include the celebrant, the reader with the book of Scriptures, and the servers bearing the cross and lighted candles. He can advise you as to the prevailing custom.

Once the liturgy is about to begin and the music starts, take a deep breath and try not to hurry. They won't start without you.

The recessional is in reverse order of the processional.

When the rites are concluded and the music begins, the groom offers his arm to his new wife; she looks radiant; they hit it.

Walk quickly, smile and proceed to the vestibule, if that

is where the receiving line will be, or to another appointed place.

The bride and groom are followed by the best man, maid of honor, other attendants, parents of the bride, parents of the groom, relatives and other guests.

The Music

Choosing Appropriate Wedding Music

In choosing wedding music, your first responsibility is to remain faithful to the purpose and integrity of the liturgy.

This concept is not difficult to apply in other areas of our lives. Plans for a fraternity mixer are not the same as plans for a brunch honoring the new dean and her husband. The rules for soccer are different from the rules for football. We accept and delight in the differences.

Some weddings are planned as if they were theatrical productions. And, since the show is one performance only, the temptation is to pile on as much extra stuff as possible. The liturgy is likely to become buried under all the extras.

Music, unlike flowers, candles and programs, is not merely an addition to the festivities or a pleasant form of entertainment for your guests. Music echoes spoken prayer and is an integral part of the liturgy. It should be chosen with regard to the same standards we apply when choosing all liturgical prayers. Catholic liturgies are carefully designed to offer glory and honor and praise and thanksgiving to God, the source and center of your lives as individuals and as a couple. Choices of sung prayer, therefore, are limited to those expressions which glorify God rather than the two of you or your parents or the computer dating service that brought you together.

Everyone enjoys songs that evoke memories of special times in one's life. If you met and fell in love during an aerobic dance class, it is understandable that you might want to hear "Uptown Girl" as the bride approaches the altar. But how will you and your fit friends resist the impulse to step, kick, turn, grapevine to the left and can-can two three four, leaving everyone in the church completely breathless by the time the wedding party reaches the sanctuary?

And remember that what touches you will not be as

touching to others. One bride had always wanted "Sunrise, Sunset" at her wedding. At the lines "When did she get to be a beauty? When did he grow to be so tall?" the guests were amused to note that the bride (who was, in fact, quite a beauty) towered over the blushing groom, who was not very tall at all.

Many of these popular wedding tunes have been sung so often that there is no longer an ounce of sentiment left to be wrung from them. And what brings back memories to you may seem long and interminable to your father who thinks that no one since Glenn Miller has written anything worth listening to.

Another responsibility you have is to a congregation of people who still think of the bride as "our little Shirley. I remember when she played the Blessed Mother in the living crèche." How will these people react upon hearing the soloist warble, "The first time ever I lay with you, and felt your heart so close to mine"? Your wedding is not the time to glorify the wonders of premarital sex.

This does not mean that you are limited to "In Christ There Is No East Or West" and "Faith of Our Fathers." There is a wealth of music available that is both contemporary and appropriate.

For most of us, our knowledge of music is limited to whatever happens to have made the top ten for the year and a half before the wedding. There is much more music available that is both pleasing to you and appropriate to the occasion. Ask someone who regularly provides liturgical music in your parish if you can come to church one night after choir practice or between Masses on Sunday so that she or he can play some of your choices for you. These people are often willing to help you extend your musical horizons even if they are not playing at your wedding.

Perhaps there is a music store nearby that will have tapes available with some of the choices. Some parish musicians also have these tapes so you can hear what they are able to do. Ask. And if they haven't made one yet, they

might do it for you because you will not be the last bride or groom to make the request.

To ease your way into choosing liturgical music, start with Scripture. Select first the psalm you will use between the first (Old Testament) and second (New Testament) readings. Recall King David dancing before the ark of the covenant and keep in mind that his psalms were written as poems and songs. Perhaps you have a favorite psalm that would be appropriate for the occasion. One bride and groom, still rejoicing in the Easter feast that preceded their wedding, used the Easter psalm, "This is the day the Lord has made; let us rejoice and be glad in it," with a musical setting familiar in their parish. There may be hymns that you have enjoyed for years without realizing that they were psalms.

The psalm having been selected, advance directly to the remaining parts of the liturgy you might want to emphasize with music. See "Planning a Wedding Liturgy" on p. 82 for guidelines concerning music for each part of the ceremony, and the conclusion of this section for suggested selections.

What about songs that have always been your favorite but haven't yet found a home in the scheme of things? Consider using them: to begin the rehearsal, at the rehearsal dinner or reception, in church before the ceremony as the guests are being seated, or after the ceremony while guests are waiting to go through the receiving line.

Does all this help you to understand why your pastor placed his head on his desk and wept when you asked to have the theme from "Rocky" played after the exchange of vows?

Titius and Bertha Select Their Wedding Music

Music suggestions are taken from *Worship*, a hymnal and service book for Roman Catholics, third edition, GIA Publications, Inc., Chicago, 1986 [referred to as W below], and *Glory and Praise*, songs for Christian assembly, volumes 1, 2 and 3, North American Liturgy Resources, Phoenix, 1980 and 1982 [referred to as GP below].

These books are among the finest and most popular hymn books available for use in American Catholic churches Many of the hymns can be found in other hymnals and others can be reprinted for your use with the permission of the publisher.

This is by no means an exhaustive list but is intended to help you in beginning the discussion of what kinds of music will suit you and those who assemble with you on your wedding day.

Praise Hymns:

All the Ends of the Earth	GP	174
City of God		187
Immortal, Invisible, God Only Wise	W	512
All Creatures of Our God and King		520
From All That Dwell Below the Skies		521
Holy God, We Praise Thy Name		524
Joyful, Joyful, We Adore Thee		525
Praise the Lord! You Heavens, Adore Him		529
Praise My Soul, the King of Heaven		530
Lord of Our Growing Years		556

Psalms:
Among those suggested for use in the lectionary.

Psalm (33) 34:2–9:	W	36
Taste and see the goodness of the Lord		
(102) 103:1–2,8,13,17–18a:		55
My soul, give thanks to the Lord and		
bless his holy name.		
(111) 112:1–9: *The just man is a light in*		
darkness to the upright.		59
(144) 145:8–10,15,17–18: *Your kingdom is*		
everlasting; you shall reign forever.		76

Others, based on the psalms, which may be found suitable include:

All My Days	GP	2
For You Are My God		16
Glory and Praise to Our God		17
I Lift Up My Soul		23
If the Lord Does Not Build		26
Like a Seal on Your Heart		34
Sing a New Song		47
Sing to the Mountains		48
You Are Near		59
I Rejoiced		106
It's a Brand New Day		107
On Eagle's Wings		126
Psalm of the Good Shepherd		231

After the Vows or at the Preparation of the Gifts

Beginning Today	GP	183
Only This I Want		224
For the Beauty of the Earth		557
O God, Our Help in Ages Past	W	579
Love Divine, All Love Excelling		588
Where True Charity and Love Are Found		
(Ubi Caritas)		598

| What Wondrous Love Is This | | 600 |
| When Love is Found | | 745 |

See also the Praise Hymns suggested above

Communion or Post-Communion

Shepherd of Souls	W	728
At That First Eucharist		733
You Satisfy the Hungry Heart		736
I Am the Bread of Life		738

The following instrumentals are among those suitable for use. These suggestions are but a small number of those available to you. If you are unfamiliar with classical music, you might call your church organist and ask to come between services on Sunday or before or after choir rehearsal if he or she would be willing to play samples of what you might select for use on your wedding day.

Preludes:

| Aria from Concerto Grosso XII | Handel |
| Fantasia | Pachelbel |

Processional Music:

Fantasy in A Minor	Bach
Processional in G Major	Handel
Solemn Processional	Handel
Trumpet Voluntary in D Major	Purcell
Marche Nuptiale	Caron

Recessional Music:

Toccata in F Major	Buxtehude
Marche Romaine	Gounod
Chromatic Fugue	Pachelbel

Postludes:

| Fantasy in C Major | Bach |
| Fugue in C Major | Mendelssohn |

The Script

Tradition

Dear Miss Manners,
Who says there is a "right" way of doing things and a "wrong" way?
Gentle Reader,
Miss Manners does. You want to make something of it?
(Miss Manners' Guide to Excruciatingly Correct Behavior)

It's your wedding and you should do what you want to do. And I'm sure that what you want to do is offend as few people as possible.
The Almost Always Right Rev. William C. Graham

You have chosen a ceremony laden with ritual and symbolism. If this were not your preference, you would have contacted a judge, a justice of the peace or a ship's captain.

This wedding of yours has both a very private significance and a very public face. How do you approach the task of planning a liturgy that meets the requirements of the Church, the requests of relatives, and your own desires?

First a word from one of our major sponsors—tradition. Tradition, a benevolent despot, insists things be done her way just because things have always been done her way. However, tradition did not come to power spontaneously or of her own accord. Tradition governs ceremonies and rituals generated by the human need to celebrate and commemorate as members of a community. Surely we can (and do) name our children, express sorrow for sins, enter adulthood, declare love for our partner, and mourn our dead in private. But there is a common desire to share these events with others. It would be difficult if not impossible to do these things publicly without tradition to guide and shape our rituals.

For instance, can you imagine what christenings would be like if there were no pattern to follow? Maybe you would choose a convenient Sunday, bring Homer Jr. to Mass, stand up after the sign of peace and get the attention of the priest and congregation. "We just wanted everyone to know that we have a new baby, and his name is Homer Jr., and we'd like him to be accepted as a member of this Christian community. Is that O.K. with everyone? Good. Thanks."

Planning a liturgy within established guidelines is tough enough. It would be a lot harder if the priest told your parents, "I'll be there at six o'clock. You guys just let me know where you want me to stand and what you want me to say."

The customs contained in all of our rituals were included for reasons that were perfectly logical at an earlier time. Now some are delightful remnants of old superstitions, while others have real historic or liturgical significance and are not done away with lightly.

Perhaps you want it all. You've always wanted it all—the white dress, the rings, the rice, "Oh Promise Me," the whole works. Fine.

On the other hand, perhaps you or your friends or family members insist that customs that do not reflect modern reality have no place in a modern ceremony.

Maybe there are objections to the idea of a bride who is wrapped like an expensive gift and presented to a waiting groom. Some will challenge suggested Scripture readings or scorn such practices as pelting one another with rice, garters, and bouquets. (And far too few of us object to the curious custom of getting completely trashed at the bachelor party.)

Now a word from our second major sponsor—compromise. Compromise gets a good workout in planning a wedding, preparing both of you for what lies ahead for the rest of your lives.

Where your wedding is concerned, you must balance your own desires with love for your parents and a sense of history: your own desires because this is one of the biggest days in your life, love for your parents because this is one of the biggest days in their lives, and a sense of history because you are a special couple in a long line of special couples to pledge your love in this ceremony. The liturgy becomes more meaningful when you include external expressions that show you are celebrating in the same way your ancestors did and your descendants will.

As you challenge these external expressions, ask yourselves what they really mean and whether you will be able to eliminate them gracefully.

For instance, why would anyone think that the father of the bride is giving his daughter away? The Church asks both groom and bride long before the wedding to sign a statement that you enter into marriage of your own free will. Few brides object to being escorted down the aisle on the arm of a handsome man. Before you insist that the man be the groom, how do you plan to break the news to the father who has dreamed for twenty-seven years of walking down the aisle with his only daughter? Good luck.

To some of you, it seems silly to be showered with handfuls of fertility symbols as you leave the church (some of the more zealous relatives even stoop to throwing *Minute* rice, for heaven's sake). But how will you prevent or replace it? It would be in questionable Catholic taste to provide all of your guests with enough birth control pills to create the same effect. Some might suggest a bird seed substitute, but how will you communicate your wishes to your guests? Write "Bird seed only" at the bottom of your invitations? People are likely to assume that you are warning them about the reception menu.

As far as Scripture is concerned, many feminists see the need to proclaim the Scriptures exactly as written to remind us of our heritage and to demonstrate the inadequacy of human language in describing God's love.

Sometimes liturgical prayers seem inadequate, too. Perhaps they do not seem to express your understanding of the nature of God or your relationship with him. Keep in mind that the Church is charged with the overwhelming task of developing prayers that speak of the faith, hope and love of 800 million Catholics worldwide. As the Church strives to be one, holy, catholic and apostolic, her prayers used for worship must reflect unity and a common sense of purpose and belief.

Private expressions of prayer change and develop as personal faith deepens and matures. Changes in liturgical prayer take place much more slowly and deliberately because so many people are affected by the change. This is why we make room in our lives for both private and congregational prayer.

All human utterances are flawed by their very nature. We turn constantly to the Holy Spirit, in whom many see the feminine face of God, to guide us and give us patience as we struggle to pray with one voice.

If it seems necessary to do away with old customs and institute new ones, remember to choose your battles wisely. And remember that your values and convictions are more accurately and lastingly reflected in your marriage than in your wedding liturgy.

The Lofty Side of Marriage

Catholics seem to have a rather solemn view of marriage. This is reflected in the Church's use of phrases like irrevocable bond, permanent commitment, total fidelity, unbreakable oneness and holy mystery when speaking of the marriage relationship. Some may be confused about what all this really means. Beyond all the Church laws governing marriage, there ought to be an appreciation of the Church's high regard for the vocation of marriage.

If you and your beloved, or other interested parties, are looking for a short and sweet pronouncement on the Catholic theology of marriage, you need only to spend a few minutes studying the nuptial blessing. All liturgical prayers and blessings are statements about the beliefs and hopes of individuals as well as the universal Church.

What you see printed for the Church to pray is what the Church believes.

"Let us pray to the Lord for Betty and Gary . . . "
The priest begins with words so familiar that sometimes the formula fails to register, but this introduction is a significant part of the blessing. An invitation to the congregation is a reminder that marriage is not just a private event. Until this point, you might think that your feelings for each other have been a romantic secret. Now your relationship takes on a public significance that goes beyond wearing wedding rings and signing "Mr. and Mrs." in the hotel guest book. The special gift which married people enjoy becomes a sign of God's love to his people.

" . . . who come to God's altar at the beginning of their married life so that they may always be united in love for each other."

Not only is your declaration of love and commitment made before Mom, Dad, Aunt Ruth, Cousin Phil and countless other members of the Gregoria and Sosser families, it is made before God. Your vows are both public and sacred. Makes you stop and think about it a little bit, doesn't it!

"Father, to reveal the plan of your love . . . "

God, who does not use the awesome power of his love lightly or without purpose, provides within marriage a means of sharing his love. As you wonder whether you really need a wedding ceremony and a marriage license to demonstrate your love commitment, it might seem as though marriage was instituted by a shrewd entrepreneur who decided to package some of this love floating around and market it to florists, dressmakers, caterers and divorce lawyers. The Christian belief is that marriage is a gift from God who is the source of all love. As Christians you have made the joint decision not only to accept this gift, but also to cherish and nurture it all the days of your lives.

" . . . you made the union of husband and wife an image of the covenant between you and your people."

When God makes promises to his people, he doesn't fool around. A covenant is not merely a contract with an option to renew after three years. God, who remains faithful no matter how often his people fail him, asks you to remain faithful to each other in good times and in bad. Because married love is a sign of God's undying love, you promise permanence as well as love to one another.

"In the fulfillment of this sacrament, the marriage of a Christian man and woman is a sign of the marriage of Christ and the Church."

All sacraments are outward expressions of God's love. Marriage remains a sacrament not just on your wedding day but on every day of your married life. As Christ ministers to his people through the Church, you constantly minister to one another and become witnesses of God's love through the sacrament of matrimony.

It is especially appropriate to note that you are the ministers of the sacrament on the wedding day with the priest as a witness. After the wedding, you will minister the sacrament daily in your new vocation as husband and wife.

And what a fun and challenging ministry it can be. The fulfillment of the sacrament begins with the exchange of vows and continues as you argue over wallpaper patterns, make love while the kids are watching cartoons, plan your dream vacation, volunteer at the food shelf together, comfort and encourage each other in times of sadness, celebrate together in times of joy, and forgive each other again and again, building and strengthening your friendship day after day.

"Lord, grant that as they begin to live this sacrament they may share with each other the gifts of your love and become one in heart and mind as witnesses to your presence in their marriage."

You will not always feel the presence of God in your marriage. At times you will feel as though the First Federal Savings and Loan has more of a presence in your marriage than God does. Occasionally God will seem temporarily out of town as you struggle to live with a teething two year old, a half-remodeled kitchen or an elderly relative.

As Christian people, you come to the altar of God to ask his blessing on your marriage. You are reminded by the Church to turn constantly toward God so that his love may be reflected in your sacrament.

"Help them create a home together and give them children to be formed by the gospel and to have a place in your family."

Many people hear this line and pounce. "Aha! That's all the Church *really* cares about! Babies! Those celibate men in

Rome can't wait till she starts turning out potential parishioners."

The Church recognizes that marriage has its own dignity for the partners while they are husband and wife as well as when they become mom and dad. The careful wording of this part of the blessing indicates that, though the other purposes of marriage are not to be considered less important, children are also gifts from God to parents who become co-creators with him.

God relies on the cooperative love of a man and a woman to enlarge his family. And he trusts that your vow of permanent love will ensure a stable, loving environment for your family, when it includes just the two of you and when it grows to include children.

"Give your blessings to Betty, your daughter, so that she may be a good wife and mother, caring for the home, faithful in love for her husband, generous and kind."

The nuptial blessing used to be called the bride's blessing and it ended here. Through this, the Church seemed to teach that the bride had a long hard road ahead of her and she was going to need all the help she could get.

This part of the blessing recalls the bride's baptism, and her own considerable dignity as a daughter of God. It also lists prominent examples of the virtues of the holy women whose praises are sung in the Scriptures.

"Give your blessing to Gary, your son, so that he may be a faithful husband and a good father."

Does the groom get cheated here? After petitioning for blessings on the bride, is the Church asking God a bit less for the guy standing next to her? Maybe the people writing the prayer figured it's hard enough just being a faithful husband and good father. And in twentieth century America, they may be right. But it also seems to be taken for granted that a faithful husband will also be generous and kind and care for the home.

"Father, grant that as they come together to your table on earth, so they may one day have the joy of sharing your feast in heaven."

Sacraments give the grace and strength needed for the journey until God's people are united with him in heaven. This is one of the strongest statements of faith you can make as individuals and as a couple. The delight you find in one another is but a brief taste and promise of what waits for you at the banquet in the new and heavenly Jerusalem.

These blessings are not bestowed on you by the Church; rather the Church joins with your friends and family in asking God to grant these many blessings. And, as do all faithful Christians, ". . . we ask this through Christ our Lord. Amen."

Planning a Wedding Liturgy

Every week, Catholics all over America "go to church." Most of us don't talk about celebrating the Eucharist, joining the assembly to greet the Lord present in word and sacrament, or participating in the saving mysteries as God's priestly people.

So when wedding time rolls around and we are invited to "plan a liturgy," pulses might quicken and stomachs tighten in anticipation of an activity that is usually reserved for experienced professionals.

Priests, deacons and liturgical musicians spend years in preparation for the job of planning and leading worship services. There is no reason that you should feel entirely and immediately comfortable in taking on the role of liturgy planner of the hour.

The amount of planning you can do will depend largely on your willingness to enter into the process coupled with parish custom and the willingness of your priest to be open to your participation.

Bride and groom come together in a church to speak their vows. Bride and groom should share in the opportunity to plan the liturgy that surrounds those vows.

Remember, as you begin the process that the bride and groom confer the sacrament upon one another as they pledge their love before the altar of God. You plan this liturgical moment insofar as you are able to select Scripture, prayers, blessings, and music that will help both you and the assembly clearly understand and celebrate the sacrament of matrimony.

As you rejoice in your love and invite the assembly to rejoice with you, remember also that you come together in praise of God and in thanksgiving for the gift of the love you have found and fashioned. It is always God who is worshiped and praised, not the bridal couple.

Perhaps the best place to begin is with Scripture. Together read the Scripture passages appointed for use during the wedding liturgy. Together read the comments provided. Discuss your favorites and give reasons for your choices. Point out to one another those ideas you consider objectionable to you. If you are uneasy discussing Scripture with one another, discuss that too.

You do justice to the richness of the word of God to consider your choices well in advance of the wedding day. Read them often until they are familiar to both of you and clear choices can be made. Then, during the liturgy, the proclamation of Scripture becomes also a proclamation of what you believe, and of your hopes for married life.

Planning ahead also prevents the following conversation from taking place in the car on the way to the rehearsal:

"Good grief, we don't have the readings picked out yet!"

"I thought you were going to do that!"

"No, remember, I said I would write up the program for the printer if you would look over the prayers and readings and let me know what sounded good."

"Well, we have to have *something*. Where's that book?"

"I gave it to you to show Mom the chapter on flower girls. Where did you put it?"

"I never took it out of the car. It must be here somewhere."

"Here it is. Now let's see . . . Scripture, Scripture . . here we go."

"Hurry and pick something. We're almost there. Just don't pick the one about wives and submission. All of Grandma's friends from NOW will be there."

If you take time to study the selections and choose the readings together, you will find yourselves forever exchanging smiles when you hear the passages of Scripture that now hold special meaning for you as a couple.

Next, consider other parts of the liturgy, both spoken and sung. They are:

Processional

This selection should be an instrumental. Having a song sung while you come down the aisle calls for too many senses to be pressed into service at one time by the assembly. Liturgical processions can be lots of fun and most people want to watch the parade. Allow your musicians to play as you enter and save the singing for another moment.

For the order of the processional, see p. 58.

Hymn

An opening hymn after the bridal procession has moved into the sanctuary is a good idea for several reasons. It sets the proper tone immediately, letting the guests know that this is a sacramental encounter that they have been invited to witness. Thus they are to join in prayer for the success of this union of the bride and groom. Inviting them to sing is inviting them to pray.

This is a particularly good opportunity for those wedding parties in which all are not Catholic. If you choose a hymn that you know to be a favorite of those family members from another Church, you are sure to impress them with your thoughtfulness.

Opening Prayer

As you read the options given, try to discern what the Church suggests in the statements made in these prayers. One of the ancient maxims of the Church is *lex orandi, lex credendi*—"the law of prayer establishes the law of belief"— which is to say that if you want to discover what the Church teaches about something in particular, look carefully at the prayers assigned for use on those occasions. The Church's theology finds its very clear expression in the wedding prayers.

Old Testament Reading

Chosen and delivered to the reader well before the rehearsal. See Scripture selection on pp. 109–118.

Psalm

Choose a psalm set to music (see p. 68) which can be sung by the congregation or the soloist. The refrains to many psalms are simple tunes that can easily be sung by a congregation led by a cantor who solos the verses.

New Testament

Also chosen and delivered to the reader in advance of the rehearsal. Your celebrant will also want to know which readings you have selected. See pp. 118–130.

Alleluia

With this acclamation, the assembly greets the Gospel in song, repeating the Alleluia refrain after the cantor.

Gospel

In the Catholic tradition, the Gospel is proclaimed only by an ordained person, but, as with the other Scripture readings, you are free to choose one which reflects your feelings about the sacrament. See pp. 130–141.

Homily

The celebrant will want to prepare a homily which is a reflection on the message contained in the word of God. This is a good reason to inform him promptly of your decisions about Scripture.

Exchange of Vows

When your parents and grandparents were married, the prevailing custom was for the bride and groom to get dressed to the nines and gather their friends and family in a public place of worship. Then, when it came to the very reason for all the hoopla, they turned their backs on everyone, went into a huddle with the priest, mumbled a few words, and that was it. They were hitched. The backs of bridal gowns are so lovely because traditionally that was all anyone ever got to see during the wedding.

Today's brides and grooms are encouraged to display

their nervous but smiling faces for all to see as they exchange vows and rings.

After all, this is where it all comes together. This is where months of preparation and planning meet a lifetime of better and worse, sickness and health, good times and bad. You want people to pay attention to this sacred moment, and they want to see and hear what's going on.

Therefore more and more priests are suggesting that when you exchange vows, you turn slightly toward one another while facing the congregation. The priest stands between the two front pews and witnesses your exchange along with the rest of the congregation who will appreciate a clear view of the main event.

Next, you will have to decide how to recite your vows. It's another one of those details that seems so simple when you watch someone else do it (after all, how hard can it be to memorize forty words?), and you want it to look that way when you do it too.

If you choose to memorize and recite them one to another, the priest will be there with his book open to the right page in the event that your memory stumbles.

You might also choose to read the vows directly from the book.

Or you can let the priest ask the traditional questions to which you reply "I do."

Which option is preferable depends largely on your personalities. If you can memorize or read well, it would certainly be appropriate to proclaim the vows to each other since you confer the sacrament on one another. In this way, your effort adds emphasis to the holy words you speak.

If the very thought of reading or speaking in public causes endless distress, play it safe and choose to respond "I do" in response to the priest's questions.

Repeating the vows line by line after the priest is usually not a good choice. It vaguely suggests that neither of you can read.

In all cases, remain sensitive to the feelings of your

partner. If what you would like to do most is something that she or he is unable to do, this is one more opportunity for you to compromise, or give in, cheerfully. ("I'll memorize the vows if you write all the thank-you notes and polish the silver twice a year" is *not* a compromise!)

Few couples ask to write their own vows because what they end up with is a longer more complicated version of the simple and noble promises prescribed by the Church. Some priests will allow you to add a sentence or two. Most are convinced that the vows as they are written are almost impossible to improve upon.

The two choices of vows for Catholics in the United States are printed on p. 96. Study them carefully and talk with your priest about which vows you have chosen and how you would like to exchange them.

Blessing and Exchanging of Rings

The symbolic significance of your wedding rings finds its expression in the prayer of blessing over them. If you ever wonder what the Church teaches about anything in particular, look for the prayers provided to be said at the time or over the objects in question.

Over the rings the priest says, "May the Lord bless these rings which you give to each other as signs of your love and fidelity."

The rings should get into the church in the best man's right front pocket. Tell him to take the rings out of the box first.

The maid of honor should probably not carry the rings. She usually doesn't have pockets and is busy enough carrying her own flowers and fixing the bridal train. The maid of honor also takes care of the bride's flowers as the vows are recited.

Some want a ring bearer. Fine. Tell your mother not to use her best Girl Scout knot tying the rings onto the pillow. More than one keepsake has been destroyed that way and more than two rings have been sent accidentally flying across the church while being pried from a tightly tied knot. A bow will hold them nicely.

Before the ceremony, the bride puts her engagement ring on her right hand. This leaves her left ring finger free to receive her wedding band from her beloved, after which she will lovingly give him his ring in the same way. Later, the engagement ring is moved to its permanent home outside the wedding band. The idea is that a vein runs directly from that finger to the heart, and if it keeps you thinking of your beloved and the sanctity of your vows, who is to dismiss the idea?

Your fingers may not fit the rings as well on the wedding day as they did when you first tried them on. The ring may require a bit of tugging to get it where it belongs. When you slip it onto your beloved's finger, push it only as far as the second knuckle if the fit is snug. Then that sweaty hand can retreat to its owner who will discreetly push the ring the rest of the way. No need for the congregation to see your first struggle when you have been married all of ninety seconds.

Before selecting music for this important moment in the liturgy, reread the actual vows and the formula for the blessing and exchange of rings. Take note of the noble simplicity of this rite. You do not want to overshadow your promises with lyrics that are trite or not in keeping with the theology of the vows.

The Kiss

After the exchange of vows and rings, you may wish to exchange a kiss. Ask the priest if this is customary in your area.

If so, the bride might not want the priest to say to the groom, "You may now kiss the bride." After all, the groom has probably not asked for priestly permission up until this point. And, if he can offer her kiss to her new husband, to whom else may he offer a kiss of hers? "You may now kiss the groom"? Not much better.

"You may now exchange a kiss" is a good statement which indicates that the kiss puts a seal on what has already been spoken. The kiss also calls to mind that marriages must be both *ratum et consummatum*, which is to say both ratified (which you do through your vows) and consummated (which usually needs little prompting from the Church).

The kiss is not to be a lengthy demonstration of what is to follow as soon as the guests go home. Some priests have been heard to suggest: "You may now exchange a chaste kiss."

Presentation and Preparation of the Gifts

If the Eucharist is celebrated, the gifts of bread and wine may be presented by the family or friends to the priest. This activity may be accompanied by a hymn. Instrumental music is suggested if a vocal solo was used after the vows.

Preface

If the Eucharist will be celebrated within the wedding liturgy, you will need to select, or have selected for you, a preface which begins the eucharistic prayer. From the options found on page 100–102, determine which most clearly expresses what you understand yourselves to be about as you begin married life.

Many people consider it awkward to ask Catholics to kneel and all others to sit during the eucharistic prayer. And it would seem not quite polite to tell those who are not Catholic, "Well, when in Rome . . . " Some suggest that all of these considerations are best met by inviting the entire congregation to stand throughout the eucharistic prayer. An ancient custom might be invoked which forbids kneeling on days of great joy; and, you might point out, standing is the posture of the resurrection people. Discuss this with the priest.

Acclamations during the Eucharistic Prayer

Musical settings for the acclamations during the eucharistic prayer should also be selected with care. These are the Holy, Holy, the Memorial Acclamation, and the Amen. Your best bet here might be to seek out your parish musician and find out which settings are most commonly sung in your parish. Stick with these. At least the guests from your home church will know these important parts of the common prayer. If the soloist is not familiar with the acclamations, insist that she or he learn them so that the congregation can have a leader.

Lord's Prayer

The Lord's Prayer is the only prayer which Jesus gave us. Christians are called to make this prayer daily, and whenever the Church gathers, it is said in unison. It can never be taken from the assembly. Therefore, it is inappropriate to have it sung as a solo during your wedding. Also, it might be the only prayer that the entire congregation will offer together since it is known by Christians of every denomination.

If you wish the entire congregation to sing the Lord's Prayer, select a setting which is familiar to most people in your area.

If it was soloed at your mom's wedding and she insists on having it at yours, you might suggest that it be sung either before the ceremony or during Communion in addition to being recited at the appointed time.

Nuptial Blessing

Choose the blessing from the options listed on pp. 102–106 that most clearly expresses your hopes for the union you begin as husband and wife before the altar of God.

Sign of Peace

Jesus promised us peace. Hopeful always, the assembly exchanges with one another some sign of this promise.

Communion

Will you need to appoint eucharistic ministers to assist with the distribution of Communion? Will all communicants be offered Communion from the cup? Ask what your parish customs are and what considerations you need to make. Decide also whether to have a hymn, solo or instrumental selection.

Blessing and Dismissal of the Congregation

Their happy task of witnessing your vows is now complete. The assembly is sent in peace to continue the celebration.

Recessional

Exit the church in the reverse order of the processional, led by the newly married couple and accompanied by instrumental music.

To Eucharist or Not To Eucharist

Whether or not to celebrate the Eucharist at your wedding may be a question that consumes many hours for some couples and their parents.

Are both bride and groom Catholics who worship regularly? There seems to be every reason then to ask that your vows be exchanged at Mass unless you live in an area where the shortage of priests makes this impossible.

If either the bride or the groom is not a Catholic, it can be presumed that about half of the guests will also not be Catholic. You might then observe that the Eucharist is a sign of unity. But when only half of the bridal couple and half of the congregation will approach the eucharistic table, our differences rather than our unity may find themselves highlighted. Perhaps it would be better to exchange your vows in a ceremony outside of Mass. Those Catholics who don't want to consider the sacrament of marriage outside the context of the Eucharist can perhaps be invited to a small Mass in the parish church earlier on the wedding day or the day before.

The feelings of the non-Catholic party must always be respected in this discussion even before the opinion of your grandmother.

If you choose to celebrate the Eucharist on this special day, what about those who are not Catholic come Communion time? This is not a question about separating sheep from goats, but is a question of eucharistic hospitality that Christian denominations answer differently.

Catholics teach that because the Eucharist is a sign of our unity and the Christian church is splintered today rather than united, we do not celebrate the Eucharist together.

Many Protestant denominations, on the other hand, say that precisely because the Eucharist is a sign of unity, all baptized persons are invited to celebrate it together as a sign of our hope until the day we are united as one flock with one shepherd.

One can hardly argue with either of these stands; it looks like a case of two different answers to a question with both answers correct. Since most of us are not theologians, the best course would be to listen to the teachings of our own Church and to respect the practices of the other churches into which we are invited.

Some people will tell you that all who participate in a Catholic wedding are expected to receive Communion. This is obviously untrue and contrary to Catholic practice. How would you like to be a Jew invited to a Catholic wedding and have that twist thrown at you?

It is best to discuss these issues with your priest. He can help you better to understand Catholic practice and where and how it differs from practices of the other churches in your area. He can also help you to interpret particular guidelines in your church which may differ in their emphases from diocese to diocese.

The Rite of Marriage

All stand, including the bride and bridegroom, and the priest addresses them in these or similar words:

My dear friends, you have come together in this church so that the Lord may seal and strengthen your love in the presence of the Church's minister and this community. Christ abundantly blesses this love. He has already consecrated you in baptism and now he enriches and strengthens you by a special sacrament so that you may assume the duties of marriage in mutual and lasting fidelity. And so, in the presence of the Church, I ask you to state your intentions.

The priest then questions them about their freedom of choice, faithfulness to each other, and the acceptance and upbringing of children:

N. and N., have you come here freely and without reservation to give yourselves to each other in marriage?

Will you love and honor each other as man and wife for the rest of your lives?

The following question may be omitted if, for example, the couple is advanced in years.

Will you accept children lovingly from God, and bring them up according to the law of Christ and his Church?

Each answers the questions separately.

CONSENT

The priest invites them to declare their consent.

Since it is your intention to enter into marriage, join your right hands, and declare your consent before God and his Church.

They join hands.

The bridegroom says:

I, N., take you, N., to be my wife. I promise to be true to you in good times and in bad, in sickness and in health. I will love you and honor you all the days of my life.

The bride says:

I, N., take you, N., to be my husband. I promise to be true to you in good times and in bad, in sickness and in health. I will love you and honor you all the days of my life.

If, however, it seems preferable for pastoral reasons, the priest may obtain consent from the couple through questions. First he asks the bridegroom:

N., do you take N. to be your wife? Do you promise to be true to her in good times and in bad, in sickness and in health, to love her and honor her all the days of your life?

The bridegroom: **I do.**

Then he asks the bride:

N., do you take N. to be your husband? Do you promise to be true to him in good times and in bad, in sickness and in health, to love him and honor him all the days of your life?

The bride: **I do.**

In the dioceses of the United States, the following form may also be used:

I, N., take you, N., for my lawful wife, to have and to hold, from this day forward, for better, for worse, for richer, for poorer, in sickness and in health, until death do us part.

I, N., take you N., for my lawful husband, to have and to hold, from this day forward, for better, for worse, for richer, for poorer, in sickness and in health, until death do us part.

If it seems preferable for pastoral reasons for the priest to obtain consent from the couple through questions, in the dioceses of the United States the following alternative form may be used:

N., do you take N. for your lawful wife (husband), to have and to hold, from this day forward, for better, for worse, for richer, for poorer, in sickness and in health, until death do you part?

The bride (bridegroom): **I do.**

Receiving their consent, the priest says:

You have declared your consent before the Church. May the Lord in his goodness strengthen your consent and fill you both with his blessings.

What God has joined, men must not divide.
℟. Amen.

BLESSING AND EXCHANGE OF RINGS

Priest:

May the Lord bless ✠ these rings which you give to each other as the sign of your love and fidelity.
℟. Amen.

Or:

Lord, bless these rings which we bless ✠ in your name.
Grant that those who wear them
may always have a deep faith in each other.
May they do your will
and always live together
in peace, good will, and love.

We ask this through Christ our Lord.
℟. Amen.

Or:

Lord,
bless ✠ and consecrate N. and N.
in their love for each other.
May these rings be a symbol

of true faith in each other,
and always remind them of their love.

We ask this through Christ our Lord.
℟. Amen.

The bridegroom places his wife's ring on her ring finger.
He may say:

N., take this ring as a sign of my love and fidelity. In the name of the Father, and of the Son, and of the Holy Spirit.

The bride places her husband's ring on his ring finger.
She may say:

N., take this ring as a sign of my love and fidelity. In the name of the Father, and of the Son, and of the Holy Spirit.

OPENING PRAYERS

Father,
you have made the bond of marriage
a holy mystery,
a symbol of Christ's love for his Church.
Hear our prayers for N. and N.
With faith in you and in each other
they pledge their love today.
May their lives always bear witness
to the reality of that love.

We ask this through our Lord Jesus Christ, your Son,
who lives and reigns with you and the Holy Spirit,
one God, for ever and ever.

Or:

Father,
hear our prayers for N. and N.,
who today are united in marriage before your altar.
Give them your blessing.
and strengthen their love for each other.

We ask this through our Lord Jesus Christ, your Son,
who lives and reigns with you and the Holy Spirit,
one God, for ever and ever.

Or:

Almighty God,
hear our prayers for N. and N.,
who have come here today
to be united in the sacrament of marriage.
Increase their faith in you and in each other,
and through them bless your Church (with Christian
   children).

We ask this through our Lord Jesus Christ, your Son,
who lives and reigns with you and the Holy Spirit,
one God, for ever and ever.

Or:

Father,
when you created mankind
you willed that man and wife should be one.
Bind N. and N.
in the loving union of marriage;
and make their love fruitful
so that they may be living witnesses
to your divine love in the world.

We ask this through our Lord Jesus Christ, your Son,
who lives and reigns with you and the Holy Spirit,
one God, for ever and ever.

PRAYERS OVER THE GIFTS

Lord,
accept our offering
for this newly-married couple, N. and N.

By your love and providence you have brought them
    together;
now bless them all the days of their married life.
We ask this through Christ our Lord.

    Or:

Lord,
accept the gifts we offer you
on this happy day.
In your fatherly love
watch over and protect N. and N.,
whom you have united in marriage.
We ask this through Christ our Lord.

    Or:

Lord,
hear our prayers
and accept the gifts we offer for N. and N.
Today you have made them one in the sacrament of
    marriage.
May the mystery of Christ's unselfish love,
which we celebrate in this eucharist,
increase their love for you and for each other.
We ask this through Christ our Lord.

PREFACES

Father, all-powerful and ever-living God,
we do well always and everywhere to give you
    thanks.
By this sacrament your grace unites man and woman
in an unbreakable bond of love and peace.

You have designed the chaste love of husband and
    wife
for the increase both of the human family
and of your own family born in baptism.

You are the loving Father of the world of nature;
you are the loving Father of the new creation of grace.
In Christian marriage you bring together the two
    orders of creation:
nature's gift of children enriches the world
and your grace enriches also your Church.

Through Christ the choirs of angels
and all the saints
praise and worship your glory.
May our voices blend with theirs
as we join in their unending hymn:

     Or:

Father, all-powerful and ever-living God,
we do well always and everywhere to give you thanks
through Jesus Christ our Lord.

Through him you entered into a new covenant with
    your people.
You restored man to grace in the saving mystery of
    redemption.
You gave him a share in the divine life
through his union with Christ.
You made him an heir of Christ's eternal glory.

This outpouring of love in the new covenant of grace
is symbolized in the marriage covenant
that seals the love of husband and wife
and reflects your divine plan of love.

And so, with the angels and all the saints in heaven
we proclaim your glory
and join in their unending hymn of praise:

Or:

Father, all-powerful and ever-living God,
we do well always and everywhere to give you
thanks.

You created man in love to share your divine life.
We see his high destiny in the love of husband
and wife,
which bears the imprint of your own divine love.

Love is man's origin,
love is his constant calling,
love is his fulfillment in heaven.

The love of man and woman
is made holy in the sacrament of marriage,
and becomes the mirror of your everlasting love.

Through Christ the choirs of angels
and all the saints
praise and worship your glory.
May our voices blend with theirs
as we join in their unending hymn:

NUPTIAL BLESSINGS

I.

My dear friends, let us turn to the Lord and pray
that he will bless with his grace this woman (or N.)
now married in Christ to this man (or N.)
and that (through the sacrament of the body and
blood of Christ,)
he will unite in love the couple he has joined in this
holy bond.

All pray silently for a short while. Then the priest
extends his hands and continues:

Father, by your power you have made everything out
of nothing.

In the beginning you created the universe
and made mankind in your own likeness.
You gave man the constant help of woman
so that man and woman should no longer be two,
    but one flesh,
and you teach us that what you have united
may never be divided.
Father, you have made the union of man and wife so
    holy a mystery
that it symbolizes the marriage of Christ and his
    Church.
Father, by your plan man and woman are united,
and married life has been established
as the one blessing that was not forfeited by original
    sin
or washed away in the flood.

Look with love upon this woman, your daughter,
now joined to her husband in marriage.
She asks your blessing.
Give her the grace of love and peace.
May she always follow the example of the holy
    women
whose praises are sung in the scriptures.

May her husband put his trust in her
and recognize that she is his equal
and the heir with him to the life of grace.
May he always honor her and love her
as Christ loves his bride, the Church.

Father, keep them always true to your
    commandments.
Keep them faithful in marriage
and let them be living examples of Christian life.

Give them the strength which comes from the gospel
so that they may be witnesses of Christ to others.
(Bless them with children
and help them to be good parents.

May they live to see their children's children.)
And, after a happy old age,
grant them fullness of life with the saints
in the kingdom of heaven.
We ask this through Christ our Lord.
℟. Amen.

II.

Let us pray to the Lord for N. and N.
who come to God's altar at the beginning of their
    married life
so that they may always be united in love for each
    other
(as now they share in the body and blood of Christ).

    All pray silently for a short while. Then the priest
extends his hands and continues:

Holy Father, you created mankind in your own image
and made man and woman to be joined as husband
    and wife
in union of body and heart
and so fulfill their mission in this world.

Father, to reveal the plan of your love,
you made the union of husband and wife
an image of the covenant between you and your
    people.
In the fulfillment of this sacrament,
the marriage of Christian man and woman
is a sign of the marriage between Christ and the
    Church.

Father, stretch out your hand, and bless N. and N.

Lord, grant that as they begin to live this sacrament
they may share with each other the gifts of your love
and become one in heart and mind
as witnesses to your presence in their marriage.
Help them to create a home together

(and give them children to be formed by the gospel
and to have a place in your family).

Give your blessings to N., your daughter,
so that she may be a good wife (and mother),
caring for the home,
faithful in love for her husband,
generous and kind.
Give your blessings to N., your son,
so that he may be a faithful husband
(and a good father).
Father, grant that as they come together to your table
 on earth,
so they may one day have the joy of sharing your feast
 in heaven.

We ask this through Christ our Lord.
℞. Amen.

III.

My dear friends, let us ask God
for his continued blessings upon this bridegroom and
 his bride (or N. and N.).

All pray silently for a short while. Then the priest
extends his hands and continues:

Holy Father, creator of the universe,
maker of man and woman in your own likeness,
source of blessing for married life,
we humbly pray to you for this woman
who today is united with her husband in this
 sacrament of marriage.

May your fullest blessing come upon her and her
 husband
so that they may together rejoice in your gift of
 married love
(and enrich your Church with their children).

Lord, may they both praise you when they are happy
and turn to you in their sorrows.
May they be glad that you help them in their work
and know that you are with them in their need.
May they pray to you in the community of the
    Church,
and be your witnesses in the world.
May they reach old age in the company of their
    friends,
and come at last to the kingdom of heaven.
We ask this through Christ our Lord.
℞. Amen.

PRAYERS AFTER COMMUNION

Lord,
in your love
you have given us this eucharist
to unite us with one another and with you.
As you have made N. and N.
one in this sacrament of marriage
(and in the sharing of the one bread and the one cup),
so now make them one in love for each other.
We ask this through Christ our Lord.

    Or:
Lord,
we who have shared the food of your table
pray for our friends N. and N.,
whom you have joined together in marriage.
Keep them close to you always.
May their love for each other
proclaim to all the world
their faith in you.
We ask this through Christ our Lord.

Or:

**Almighty God,
may the sacrifice we have offered
and the eucharist we have shared
strengthen the love of N. and N.,
and give us all your fatherly aid.**

We ask this through Christ our Lord.

BLESSING AT THE END OF MASS

**God the eternal Father keep you in love with each
    other,
so that the peace of Christ may stay with you
and be always in your home.**
℞. **Amen.**

**May (your children bless you,)
your friends console you
and all men live in peace with you.**
℞. **Amen.**

**May you always bear witness to the love of God in
    this world
so that the afflicted and the needy
will find in you generous friends,
and welcome you into the joys of heaven.**
℞. **Amen.**

**And may almighty God bless you all,
the Father, and the Son, ✠ and the Holy Spirit.**
℞. **Amen.**

Or:

**May God, the almighty Father,
give you his joy
and bless you (in your children).**
℞. **Amen.**

May the only Son of God have mercy on you
and help you in good times and in bad.
℞. Amen.

May the Holy Spirit of God
always fill your hearts with his love.
℞. Amen.

And may almighty God bless you all,
the Father, and the Son, ✠ and the Holy Spirit.
℞. Amen.

Or:

May the Lord Jesus, who was a guest at the wedding
   in Cana,
bless you and your families and friends.
℞. Amen.

May Jesus, who loved his Church to the end,
always fill your hearts with his love.
℞. Amen.

May he grant that, as you believe in his resurrection,
so you may wait for him in joy and hope.
℞. Amen.

And may almighty God bless you all,
the Father, and the Son, ✠ and the Holy Spirit.
℞. Amen.

Selecting the Readings

Read all of the Scripture passages reprinted in this section which are appointed for use at the wedding liturgy. Read the comments provided. Discuss your favorites and give your reasons one to another. Also point out to one another those ideas you consider alien or difficult, remembering that Jesus often speaks to his Church about things we choose not to hear in ways we consider hard to follow. Then consider that the Scriptures are not a supermarket where you choose what you like while leaving the rest on the shelves. All of Scripture is for our consideration and helps to form us as it has formed the Church and our ancestors in the faith these past two thousand years.

As you read these Scriptures and consider their significance, you do well to rejoice in being part of something far bigger than yourselves. These insights, commands, gentle suggestions and stories are what will make God part of your union, and your love the very presence on earth in tangible and visible ways of the perfecting love of God.

There are many translations of the Bible available today. Because familiarity helps us grow in our appreciation of the word of God, the translation printed here is the same one used in the Catholic churches in the United States.

 OLD TESTAMENT READINGS

Genesis 1:26–28,31a

In creating humankind and in the command to multiply and fill the earth, God invites men and women to be co-creators with him in building the earthly city. In accepting the invitation, you participate in a form of love that stretches back to the beginning of time and, through you, stretches into the future.

A reading from the book of Genesis
[*Male and female he created them.*]

God said: "Let us make man in our image, after our likeness. Let them have dominion over the fish of the sea, the birds of the air, and the cattle, and over all the wild animals and all the creatures that crawl on the ground."

God created man in his image;
in the divine image he created him;
male and female he created them.

God blessed them, saying: "Be fertile and multiply, fill the earth and subdue it. Have dominion over the fish of the sea, the birds of the air, and all the living things that move on the earth." God looked at everything he had made, and he found it very good.

This is the Word of the Lord.

♥

Genesis 2:18–24

Eve is created from the side of Adam. Because man and woman are created from the same stuff, they are equal in status and dignity.

In managing the peaceable kingdom, the first man needed help. Head of the household is still a big job for one person to handle alone. Husband and wife, with different talents and interests, complement each other and together meet the challenges of family life.

A reading from the book of Genesis
[And they will be two in one flesh.]

The Lord God said: "It is not good for the man to
be alone. I will make a suitable partner for him."
So the Lord God formed out of the ground various
wild animals and various birds of the air, and he
brought them to the man to see what he would call
them; whatever the man called each of them would
be its name. The man gave names to all the cattle,
all the birds of the air, and all the wild animals; but
none proved to be the suitable partner for the man.

So the Lord God cast a deep sleep on the man,
and while he was asleep, he took out one of his ribs
and closed up its place with flesh. The Lord God
then built up into a woman the rib that he had
taken from the man. When he brought her to the
man, the man said:

"This one, at last, is bone of my bones
and flesh of my flesh;
This one shall be called 'woman,'
for out of 'her man' this one has been
taken."

That is why a man leaves his father and mother and
clings to his wife, and the two of them become one
body.

This is the Word of the Lord.

♥

Genesis 24:48–51,58–67

Isaac and Rebekah give themselves freely, one to
another, in marriage. (See also the commentary for the
following selection from Tobit.)

Marriage vows, like baptismal and confirmation
promises, are usually spoken at a time when those involved
cannot possibly realize the extent of what will be required of

111

them as Christian people. Engaged couples often ask married people which years are the hardest. Any couple who gets past the first anniversary knows that the years are easy but the days are tough. If you plan to live another forty years, "all the days of your life" add up to at least 14,610 days. Like Rebekah and Isaac, you dedicate yourselves to each other with innocent faithfulness and boundless love.

A reading from the book of Genesis
[Isaac loved Rebekah, and so he was consoled for the loss of his mother.]

The servant of Abraham said to Laban: "I bowed down in worship to the Lord, blessing the Lord, the God of my master Abraham, who had led me on the right road to obtain the daughter of my master's kinsman for his son. If, therefore, you have in mind to show true loyalty to my master, let me know; but if not, let me know that, too. I can then proceed accordingly."

Laban and his household said in reply: "This thing comes from the Lord; we can say nothing to you either for or against it. Here is Rebekah, ready for you; take her with you, that she may become the wife of your master's son, as the Lord has said."

So they called Rebekah and asked her, "Do you wish to go with this man?" She answered, "I do." At this they allowed their sister Rebekah and her nurse to take leave, along with Abraham's servant and his men. Invoking a blessing on Rebekah, they said:
"Sister, may you grow
  into thousands of myriads;
And may your descendants gain possession
  of the gates of their enemies!"
Then Rebekah and her maids started out; they mounted their camels and followed the man. So the servant took Rebekah and went on his way.

Meanwhile Isaac had gone from Beer-lahairoi and was living in the region of the Negeb. One day toward evening he went out . . . in the field, and as he looked around, he noticed that camels were approaching. Rebekah, too, was looking about, and when she saw him, she alighted from her camel and asked the servant, "Who is the man out there, walking through the fields toward us?" "That is my master," replied the servant. Then she covered herself with her veil.

The servant recounted to Isaac all the things he had done. Then Isaac took Rebekah into his tent; he married her, and thus she became his wife. In his love for her Isaac found solace after the death of his mother Sarah.

This is the Word of the Lord.

♥

Tobit 7:9c–10,11c–17

You are strangers in many ways as you commit yourselves to the lifelong marriage relationship. You marry a young man or woman. Years from now, you may be married to a mother, a father, a grandparent, a person with a different career, a retired person. This reading and the preceding selection from Genesis illustrate the enormous faith you place in one another and in the awesome power of your love.

A reading from the book of Tobit
[*May God join you together and fill you with his blessings.*]

Tobiah said to Raphael, "Brother Azariah, ask Raguel to let me marry my kinswoman Sarah." Raguel overheard the words; so he said to the boy: "Eat and drink and be merry tonight, for no man is more entitled to marry my daughter Sarah than you, brother. Besides, not even I have the right to give her to anyone but you, because you are my closest relative. But I will explain the situation to you very frankly. She is yours according to the decree of the Book of Moses. Your marriage to her has been decided in heaven! Take your kinswoman; from now on you are her love, and she is your beloved. She is yours today and ever after. And tonight, son, may the Lord of heaven prosper you both. May he grant you mercy and peace." Then Raguel called his daughter Sarah, and she came to him. He took her by the hand and gave her to Tobiah with the words: "Take her according to the law. According to the decree written in the Book of Moses she is your wife. Take her and bring her back safely to your father. And may the God of heaven grant both of you peace and prosperity." He then called her mother and told her to bring a scroll, so that he might draw up a marriage contract stating that he gave Sarah to Tobiah as his wife according to the decree of the Mosaic law. Her mother brought the scroll, and he drew up the contract, to which they affixed their seals.

Afterward they began to eat and drink.
This is the Word of the Lord.

Tobit 8:4–9

Imagine how thrilled Sarah must have been with her husband's request at the end of a long, hard day. "You want to do what? Pray! Do you have any idea what time it is? Can't we pray in the morning?"

Of course Tobiah knows what time it is, but he is so filled with love for his God and his wife that his expression of love can't wait. In this moving prayer, he asks God to bless his wife. He asks also for a long life with her, a wish he may have found unfulfilled if he hadn't let her get some rest.

A reading from the book of Tobit
[May God bring us to old age together.]

On the wedding night Sarah got up, and she and
Tobiah started to pray and beg that deliverance
might be theirs. He began with these words:
"Blessed are you, O God of our fathers;
  praised be your name forever and ever.
Let the heavens and all your creation
  praise you forever.
You made Adam and you gave him his wife
    Eve
  to be his help and support;
  and from these two the human race de-
    scended.
You said, 'It is not good for the man to be
    alone;
  let us make him a partner like himself.'
Now, Lord, you know that I take this wife of
    mine
  not because of lust,
  but for a noble purpose.
Call down your mercy on me and on her,
  and allow us to live together to a happy old
    age."
This is the Word of the Lord.

♥

Song of Songs 2:8–10,14,16a;8:6–7a

The Canticle, attributed to King Solomon, is the only
book from which no reading is appointed for use during the
three year cycle of Sunday readings. The reason, perhaps, is
that the scriptural author freely uses sexual imagery to speak
of love's ecstasy. The manner is so straightforward, the
imagery so erotic, that those who selected the Sunday
readings may have thought this spiritual canticle entirely too
much for us.

115

We know that women in ancient times were treated as slaves or property and remained bound to a relationship out of economic necessity. Yet here is a woman who would fit right into the plot of a romance novel. This description of love is as passionate, sensual and exhilarating as Tobias' is spiritual.

A reading from the Song of Songs
[For love is as strong as death.]

Hark! my lover—here he comes
　　springing across the mountains,
　　leaping across the hills.
My lover is like a gazelle
　　or a young stag.
Here he stands behind our wall,
　　gazing through the windows,
　　peering through the lattices.
My lover speaks; he says to me,
　　"Arise, my beloved, my beautiful one,
　　and come!

"O my dove in the clefts of the rock,
　　in the secret recesses of the cliff,
Let me see you,
　　let me hear your voice,
For your voice is sweet,
　　and you are lovely."
My lover belongs to me and I to him.
　　[He said to me:]
Set me as a seal on your heart,
　　as a seal on your arm;
For stern as death is love,
　　relentless as the nether world is devotion;
　　its flames are a blazing fire.
Deep waters cannot quench love,
　　nor floods sweep it away.
　　　　　　This is the Word of the Lord.

Sirach 26:1–4,16–21

The perfect wife is described here; the perfect husband isn't. In reality, neither one exists. Anyone who sponsors a talent search for Mr. or Ms. Right is destined for disappointment. The perfect spouse is one who, over the years, becomes sensitive to the other's needs, shares triumphs and challenges, and is willing to compromise. Life is rich and full when shared with such a spouse.

A reading from the book of Sirach
[Like the sun rising is the beauty of a good wife in a well-kept house.]

Happy the husband of a good wife,
　twice-lengthened are his days;
A worthy wife brings joy to her husband,
　peaceful and full is his life.
A good wife is a generous gift
　bestowed upon him who fears the Lord;
Be he rich or poor, his heart is content,
　and a smile is ever on his face.
A gracious wife delights her husband,
　her thoughtfulness puts flesh on his bones;
A gift from the Lord is her governed speech,
　and her firm virtue is of surpassing worth.
Choicest of blessings is a modest wife,
　priceless her chaste person.
Like the sun rising in the Lord's heavens,
　the beauty of a virtuous wife is the radiance of
　　her home.
This is the Word of the Lord.

Jeremiah 31:31–32a,33–34a

The covenant that God enters with his people is the model for the covenant of marriage. Marriage spoken of as covenant suggests a pretty heavy-duty promise. It isn't like promising to put gas in the car or pay back a loan. In ancient times, contracts were sealed by those involved walking between the halves of freshly slaughtered animals, implying that should they not remain faithful to their promise, they should suffer the same fate as the animals. (Also giving new meaning to the question, "So what am I? Chopped liver?") Your promises are not given lightly, with little thought, or for a period of time any less lengthy than until death.

A reading from the book of the prophet Jeremiah
[I will make a new covenant with the house of Israel and Judah.]

The days are coming, says the Lord, when I will make a new covenant with the house of Israel and the house of Judah. It will not be like the covenant I made with their fathers the day I took them by the hand to lead them forth from the land of Egypt. But this is the covenant which I will make with the house of Israel after those days, says the Lord. I will place my law within them, and write it upon their hearts; I will be their God, and they shall be my people. No longer will they have need to teach their friends and kinsmen how to know the Lord. All, from least to greatest, shall know me, says the Lord.

This is the Word of the Lord.

NEW TESTAMENT READINGS

Romans 8:31b–35,37–39

Nothing can separate us from the love of God.

Your marriage begins surrounded by the sung, spoken and silent prayers of those who worship with you. You are

invited to remember to turn to God often in times of
thanksgiving, sorrow and need by tapping the limitless
resource of grace available in and through prayer.

A reading from the letter of Paul to the Romans
[Who will separate us from the love of Christ?]

If God is for us, who can be against us? Is it
possible that he who did not spare his own Son but
handed him over for the sake of us all will not grant
us all things besides? Who shall bring a charge
against God's chosen ones? God, who justifies?
Who shall condemn them? Christ Jesus, who died
or rather was raised up, who is at the right hand of
God and who intercedes for us?

Who will separate us from the love of Christ?
Trial, or distress, or persecution, or hunger, or
nakedness, or danger, or the sword? Yet in all this
we are more than conquerors because of him who
has loved us. For I am certain that neither death
nor life, neither angels nor principalities, neither
the present nor the future, nor powers, neither
height nor depth nor any other creature, will be
able to separate us from the love of God that comes
to us in Christ Jesus, our Lord.

This is the Word of the Lord.

Romans 12:1–2,9–13
or Romans 12:1–2,9–18

Paul charges us to let our behavior be changed by the
new reality which Christ brings to the world. Exercise your
patience, humility and sense of humor on each other and the
world will be a better place.

Twentieth century America can be a harsh environment
for a Christian marriage. The modern world urges self-

fulfillment while Christ demands dedication to others. Christ asks for, and promises, a love that is permanent and unconditional. The modern reality is that many couples stay together as long as things work out. Let your behavior as a Christian couple change the world rather than the other way around.

A reading from the letter of Paul to the Romans
[Offer to God your bodies as a living and holy sacrifice, truly pleasing to him.]
(Long Form)

Brothers, I beg you through the mercy of God to offer your bodies as a living sacrifice holy and acceptable to God, your spiritual worship. Do not conform yourselves to this age but be transformed by the renewal of your mind, so that you may judge what is God's will, what is good, pleasing and perfect.

Your love must be sincere. Detest what is evil, cling to what is good. Love one another with the affection of brothers. Anticipate each other in showing respect. Do not grow slack but be fervent in spirit; he whom you serve is the Lord. Rejoice in hope, be patient under trial, persevere in prayer. Look on the needs of the saints as your own; be generous in offering hospitality. Bless your persecutors; bless and do not curse them. Rejoice with those who rejoice, weep with those who weep. Have the same attitude toward all. Put away ambitious thoughts and associate with those who are lowly. Do not be wise in your own estimation. Never repay injury with injury. See that your conduct is honorable in the eyes of all. If possible, live peaceably with everyone.

This is the Word of the Lord.

Brothers, I beg you through the mercy of God to offer your bodies as a living sacrifice holy and acceptable to God, your spiritual worship. Do not conform yourselves to this age but be transformed by the renewal of your mind so that you may judge what is God's will, what is good, pleasing and perfect.

Your love must be sincere. Detest what is evil, cling to what is good. Love one another with the affection of brothers. Anticipate each other in showing respect. Do not grow slack but be fervent in spirit; he whom you serve is the Lord. Rejoice in hope, be patient under trial, persevere in prayer. Look on the needs of the saints as your own; be generous in offering hospitality.

This is the Word of the Lord.

♥

1 Corinthians 6:13c–15a,17–20

You already know that fornication is a sin. And you probably keep your temple of the Holy Spirit clean, tastefully decorated and up to code. Now use it as the architect intended.

We belong to Christ and should be aware of the dignity of our baptized bodies.

A reading from the first letter of Paul to the Corinthians
[Your body is a temple of the Spirit.]

The body is not for immorality; it is for the Lord, and the Lord is for the body. God, who raised up the Lord, will raise us also by his power. Do you not see that your bodies are members of Christ?

121

But whoever is joined to the Lord becomes one spirit with him. Shun lewd conduct. Every other sin a man commits is outside his body, but the fornicator sins against his own body. You must know that your body is a temple of the Holy Spirit, who is within—the Spirit you have received from God. You are not your own. You have been purchased, and at what a price! So glorify God in your body.

This is the Word of the Lord.

♥

1 Corinthians 12:31—13:8a

In the most popular of all wedding readings, Paul describes the look and feel of love.

The only ones who tire of this reading are priests who do over fifty weddings a year.

A reading from the first letter of Paul to the Corinthians
[If I am without love,
it will do me no good whatever.]

Set your hearts on the greater gifts. I will show you the way which surpasses all the others. If I speak with human tongues and angelic as well, but do not have love, I am a noisy gong, a clanging cymbal. If I have the gift of prophecy and, with full knowledge, comprehend all mysteries, if I have faith great enough to move mountains, but have not love, I am nothing. If I give everything I have to feed the poor and hand over my body to be burned, but have not love, I gain nothing.

Love is patient; love is kind. Love is not jealous, it does not put on airs, it is not snobbish. Love is never rude, it is not self-seeking, it is not prone to anger; neither does it brood over injuries.

Love does not rejoice in what is wrong but rejoices with the truth. There is no limit to love's forbearance, to its trust, its hope, its power to endure.

Love never fails.
This is the Word of the Lord.

Ephesians 5:2a,21–33
or Ephesians 5:2a,25–32

Paul always gets a bad rap for this one because it is often not read carefully, in its proper context or in entirety. He does not describe marriage as it ought to exist in every age, but, using the model of marriage he knew, he develops the radical notion that husbands and wives ought to treat each other with love and not as property. Paul takes Christ's revolutionary directive (love others as you love yourself) and makes it even more revolutionary by suggesting that "others" includes wives.

He uses the model of Christ's love for his bride, the Church, and suggests that human love mirror the perfect love of God. This reading is a must for feminists of either sex.

A reading from the letter of Paul to the Ephesians
[*This mystery has many implications, and I am saying it applies to Christ and the Church.*]
(Long Form)

Follow the way of love, even as Christ loved you. He gave himself for us.

Defer to one another out of reverence for Christ.

Wives should be submissive to their husbands as if to the Lord because the husband is head of his wife just as Christ is head of his body the church, as well as its savior. As the church submits to Christ, so wives should submit to their husbands in everything.

Husbands, love your wives, as Christ loved the church. He gave himself up for her to make her holy, purifying her in the bath of water by the power of the word, to present to himself a glorious church, holy and immaculate, without stain or wrinkle or anything of that sort. Husbands should love their wives as they do their own bodies. He who loves his wife loves himself. Observe that no one ever hates his own flesh; no, he nourishes it and takes care of it as Christ cares for the church—for we are members of his body.

"For this reason a man shall leave his father
    and mother,
  and shall cling to his wife,
  and the two shall be made into one."

This is a great foreshadowing; I mean that it refers to Christ and the church. In any case, each one should love his wife as he loves himself, the wife for her part showing respect for her husband.
This is the Word of the Lord.

OR

(Short Form)

Follow the way of love, even as Christ loved you. He gave himself for us.

Husbands, love your wives, as Christ loved the church. He gave himself up for her to make her holy, purifying her in the bath of water by the power of the word, to present to himself a glorious church, holy and immaculate, without stain or wrinkle or anything of that sort. Husbands should love their wives as they do their own bodies. He who loves his wife loves himself. Observe that no one ever hates his own flesh; no, he nourishes it and takes care of it as Christ cares for the church—for we are members of his body.

124

"For this reason a man shall leave his father
    and mother,
  and shall cling to his wife,
  and the two shall be made into one."
This is a great foreshadowing; I mean that it refers
to Christ and the church.
This is the Word of the Lord.

♥

Colossians 3:12–17

Paul emphasizes the dignity that is each Christian's by
virtue of baptism. He tells God's chosen people how we
ought to live. The tentmaker in Paul sees things in terms of
cloth; he suggests that over our other clothes, we put on the
garment of love.

God's blessing on your union is not duty-free. Paul tells
God's chosen people how they ought to treat each other:
with compassion, kindness, humility, gentleness, patience,
forgiveness, wisdom and gratitude. This may be difficult
when your partner is three hours late and hasn't called, or
you're stuck on the side of a four-lane highway in a car that
was supposed to have a full tank of gas.

A reading from the letter of Paul to the Colossians
[*Above all have love,
which is the bond of perfection.*]

Because you are God's chosen ones, holy and
beloved, clothe yourselves with heartfelt mercy,
with kindness, humility, meekness, and patience.
Bear with one another; forgive whatever grievances
you have against one another. Forgive as the Lord
has forgiven you. Over all these virtues put on
love, which binds the rest together and makes
them perfect. Christ's peace must reign in your
hearts, since as members of the one body you have

been called to that peace. Dedicate yourselves to
thankfulness. Let the word of Christ, rich as it is,
dwell in you. In wisdom made perfect, instruct and
admonish one another. Sing gratefully to God from
your hearts in psalms, hymns, and inspired songs.
Whatever you do, whether in speech or in action,
do it in the name of the Lord Jesus. Give thanks to
God the Father through him.

This is the Word of the Lord.

♥

1 Peter 3:1–9

The scriptural author points out that wives can win over
their husbands to the truth by proper behavior. The
assumption is that wives have first heard and been formed
by the word of God, while the men have not. Husbands,
therefore, are admonished to treat their wives with
consideration. This admonition must have been shocking to
the ears of one who believed, as society taught, that he
owned his wife.

A reading from the first letter of Peter
[*You should agree with one another, be
sympathetic and love the brothers.*]

You married women must obey your husbands, so
that any of them who do not believe in the word of
the gospel may be won over apart from preaching,
through their wives' conduct. They have only to
observe the reverent purity of your way of life. The
affectation of an elaborate hairdress, the wearing of
golden jewelry, or the donning of rich robes is not
for you. Your adornment is rather the hidden
character of the heart, expressed in the unfading
beauty of a calm and gentle disposition. This is
precious in God's eyes. The holy women of past
ages used to adorn themselves in this way, reliant

on God and obedient to their husbands—for example, Sarah, who was subject to Abraham and called him her master. You are her children when you do what is right and let no fears alarm you.

You husbands, too, must show consideration for those who share your lives. Treat women with respect as the weaker sex, heirs just as much as you to the gracious gift of life. If you do so, nothing will keep your prayers from being answered.

In summary, then, all of you should be likeminded, sympathetic, loving toward one another, kindly disposed, and humble. Do not return evil for evil or insult for insult. Return a blessing instead. This you have been called to do, that you may receive a blessing as your inheritance.
This is the Word of the Lord.

♥

1 John 3:18–24

Love proves itself not through speech but through action.

Life with Christ is not a destination at which we arrive, either here or in heaven, but a way of traveling. God wisely sees to it that we receive the guidance we need for this challenging journey. We are guided by his commandments and by the presence of the Holy Spirit in our lives.

A reading from the first letter of John
[*Our love is to be something real and active*]

Little children,
let us love in deed and in truth,
and not merely talk about it.
This is our way of knowing we are committed to the
    truth
and are at peace before him

no matter what our consciences may charge us
    with;
for God is greater than our hearts
and all is known to him.
Beloved,
if our consciences have nothing to charge us with,
we can be sure that God is with us
and that we will receive at his hands
whatever we ask.
Why? Because we are keeping his commandments
and doing what is pleasing in his sight.
His commandment is this:
we are to believe in the name of his Son, Jesus
    Christ,
and are to love one another as he commanded us.
Those who keep his commandments remain in him
and he in them.
And this is how we know that he remains in us:
from the Spirit that he gave us.

This is the Word of the Lord.

1 John 4:7–12

God has first loved us; we, therefore, ought to love one
another.

There are times in our lives when we feel so angry or
hurt or powerless that we don't feel God's presence in our
lives. But even when God seems so distant, he is present in
the love we share with others.

A reading from the first letter of John
[*God is love.*]

Beloved,
let us love one another
because love is of God;

everyone who loves is begotten of God
and has knowledge of God.
The man without love has known nothing of God,
for God is love.
God's love was revealed in our midst in this way:
he sent his only Son to the world
that we might have life through him.
Love, then, consists in this:
not that we have loved God,
but that he has loved us
and has sent his Son as an offering for our sins
Beloved,
if God has loved us so,
we must have the same love for one another
No one has ever seen God.
Yet if we love one another
God dwells in us,
and his love is brought to perfection in us
This is the Word of the Lord.

♥

Revelation 19:1,5–9a

John compares heaven to a wedding feast.

And when John dreams, he dreams big (maybe he should have skipped that large pizza with extra figs and olives before going to bed). Biblical imagery is substantially enriched because the angel in his dream thought to remind him to get it all down in writing.

Like the bride's white linen that is made of the good deeds of the saints, your wedding day is so exciting and dazzling and full of fun because of the thoughtful efforts of many loving friends and family members. Take time often to remember and pray for the people whose love and concern is woven into the fabric of your lives.

A reading from the book of Revelation
[Happy are those who are invited to the wedding feast of the Lamb.]

I, John, heard what sounded like the loud song of a great assembly in heaven. They were singing:
"Alleluia!
Salvation, glory, and might belong to our God."
A voice coming from the throne cried out:
"Praise our God, all you his servants, the small and the great, who revere him!" Then I heard what sounded like the shouts of a great crowd, or the roaring of the deep, or mighty peals of thunder, as they cried:
"Alleluia!
The Lord is king,
    our God, the Almighty!
Let us rejoice and be glad,
    and give him glory!
For this is the wedding day of the Lamb,
    his bride has prepared herself for the wedding
She has been given a dress to wear
    made of finest linen, brilliant white."
(The linen dress is the virtuous deeds of God's saints.)
The angel then said to me: "Write this down: Happy are they who have been invited to the wedding feast of the Lamb."
This is the Word of the Lord.

GOSPEL READINGS

Matthew 5:1–12a

With the crowds in the distance, Jesus addresses his disciples who gather around him. He indicates that lasting happiness is found in places where we might not first look

In the day-to-day grind of family life, it is common for us to feel that we're really not doing much to advance the kingdom of God. Christ speaks to us gently. Happy are they who resolve quarrels at home or in the office. Happy are they who do without a dinner out in order to increase their contribution to the food shelf. Happy are they who put up with resistance and complaints as they impose limits on their children.

A reading from the holy gospel according to Matthew
[Rejoice and be glad, for your reward will be great in heaven.]

When Jesus saw the crowds he went up on the mountainside. After he had sat down his disciples gathered around him, and he began to teach them:

"How blest are the poor in spirit: the reign of God is theirs.

Blest too are the sorrowing; they shall be consoled [Blest are the lowly; they shall inherit the land.] Blest are they who hunger and thirst for holiness; they shall have their fill.

Blest are they who show mercy; mercy shall be theirs.

Blest are the single-hearted for they shall see God.

Blest too the peacemakers; they shall be called sons of God.

Blest are those persecuted for holiness' sake; the reign of God is theirs.

Blest are you when they insult you and persecute you and utter every kind of slander against you because of me.

Be glad and rejoice, for your reward in heaven is great."

This is the gospel of the Lord.

Salt and light, without which life would be insipid and impossible, are compared to those faithful people who hear and put into practice the word of God. Continuing the flurry of images, the faithful are also called the light of the world. The challenge to those being married is clear. Recognize and rejoice in each other's success. Take pride in each other's accomplishments.

A reading from the holy gospel according to Matthew
[*You are the light of the world.*]

Jesus said to his disciples: "You are the salt of the earth. But what if salt goes flat? How can you restore its flavor? Then it is good for nothing but to be thrown out and trampled underfoot.

"You are the light of the world. A city set on a hill cannot be hidden. Men do not light a lamp and then put it under a bushel basket. They set it on a stand where it gives light to all in the house. In the same way, your light must shine before men so that they may see goodness in your acts and give praise to your heavenly Father."
This is the gospel of the Lord.

Matthew 7:21,24–25;
or Matthew 7:21,24–29

Marriages, like houses, must be built on firm foundations.

A good marriage is not built on one huge rock but on a whole pile of little ones. Though it might shift or settle from time to time, the foundation is secured and strengthened whenever your love for each other is expressed in simple, sincere words, like "I'm sorry," "Thank you," and "Gee, you look nice!"

A reading from the holy gospel according to Matthew
[He built his house on rock.]
(Long Form)

Jesus said to his disciples: "None of those who cry out, 'Lord, Lord,' will enter the kingdom of God but only the one who does the will of my Father in heaven.

"Anyone who hears my words and puts them into practice is like the wise man who built his house on rock. When the rainy season set in, the torrents came and the winds blew and buffeted his house. It did not collapse; it had been solidly set on rock. Anyone who hears my words but does not put them into practice is like the foolish man who built his house on sandy ground. The rains fell, the torrents came, the winds blew and lashed against his house. It collapsed under all this and was completely ruined."

Jesus finished this discourse and left the crowds spellbound at his teaching. The reason was that he taught with authority and not like the scribes.

This is the gospel of the Lord.

OR
(Short Form)

Jesus said to his disciples: "None of those who cry out, 'Lord, Lord,' will enter the kingdom of God but only the one who does the will of my Father in heaven.

"Anyone who hears my words and puts them into practice is like the wise man who built his house on rock. When the rainy season set in, the torrents came and the winds blew and buffeted his house. It did not collapse; it had been solidly set on rock."

This is the gospel of the Lord.

Matthew 19:3–6

Man and woman leave mother and father and cling to one another. What God has joined, no one must separate.

There is more to fidelity than being in the right bed at the right time. You must also promise to be loyal and supportive of each other, even at times which do not seem to be of earth-shaking significance.

A reading from the holy gospel according to Matthew
[*So then, what God has united,
man must not divide.*]

Some Pharisees came up to Jesus and said, to test him, "May a man divorce his wife for any reason whatever?" He replied, "Have you not read that at the beginning the Creator made them male and female and declared, 'For this reason a man shall leave his father and mother and cling to his wife, and the two shall become as one'? Thus they are no longer two but one flesh. Therefore, let no man separate what God has joined."

This is the gospel of the Lord.

Matthew 22:35–40

Which commandment is the greatest? Jesus answers easily the question which had been intended to trip him up He also adds a second commandment to the law. These few verses serve as a condensed version of all the scriptures.

As simple as it sounds, we know that it is difficult to live as Jesus asks. Your vows, so simple in their beauty and familiarity, will change you and challenge you every day of your married life.

A reading from the holy gospel according to Matthew
[This is the greatest and the first commandment. The second is similar to it.]

One of the Pharisees, a lawyer, in an attempt to trip up Jesus, asked him, "Teacher, which commandment of the law is the greatest?" Jesus said to him:

" 'You shall love the Lord your God
with your whole heart,
with your whole soul,
and with all your mind.'

This is the greatest and first commandment. The second is like it:

'You shall love your neighbor as yourself.'
On these two commandments the whole law is based, and the prophets as well."

This is the gospel of the Lord.

Mark 10:6–9

Mark echoes the 19th chapter of Matthew.

In marriage, the whole is definitely greater than the sum of the parts. Good marriages are never 50-50. Act as a team and not as scorekeepers.

A reading from the holy gospel according to Mark
[They are no longer two, therefore, but one body.]

Jesus said: "At the beginning of creation God made them male and female; for this reason a man shall leave his father and mother and the two shall

135

become as one. They are no longer two but one flesh. Therefore let no man separate what God has joined."

This is the gospel of the Lord.

♥

John 2:1–11

Jesus is the perfect guest: he transforms water into wine and the party continues. This is his first public miracle. Catholic people see the fact that the occurrence took place at a marriage as scriptural foundation for the sacrament of marriage. Christ blesses the marriage union and through married love lets his presence be both visible and tangible to all the world.

This really isn't a lesson on what can happen when unexpectedly prolific guests show up at the reception. Jesus heard his mother's request (thank goodness that celibates sometimes hear the suggestions of married people). You repeat the miracle daily as you become sacrament with one another. As water was changed to wine, your love for each other changes ordinary people into signs and symbols of God's presence among us on earth.

A reading from the holy gospel according to John
[*This was the first of the signs given by Jesus; it was given at Cana in Galilee.*]

There was a wedding at Cana in Galilee, and the mother of Jesus was there. Jesus and his disciples had likewise been invited to the celebration. At a certain point the wine ran out, and Jesus' mother told him, "They have no more wine." Jesus replied, "Woman, how does this concern of yours involve me? My hour has not yet come." His mother instructed those waiting on table, "Do whatever he tells you." As prescribed for Jewish ceremonial washings, there were at hand six stone water jars, each one holding fifteen to twenty-five gallons. "Fill those jars with water," Jesus ordered, at which they filled them to the brim. "Now," he said, "draw some out and take it to the waiter in charge." They did as he instructed them. The waiter in charge tasted the water made wine, without knowing where it had come from; only the waiters knew, since they had drawn the water. Then the waiter in charge called the groom over and remarked to him: "People usually serve the choice wine first; then when the guests have been drinking a while, a lesser vintage. What you have done is keep the choice wine until now." Jesus performed this first of his signs at Cana in Galilee. Thus did he reveal his glory, and his disciples believed in him.

This is the gospel of the Lord.

John 15:9–12

Just as Jesus is united to the Father in love, so also are we united one to another through him to the Father. He does not suggest, but rather commands, that his followers love one another just as he has loved.

It would seem impossible for us to demonstrate our love to the extent that Jesus did. Yet, as husbands and wives, mothers and fathers, you will be thrust into many opportunities to serve others with selfless love. The daily, mundane acts of feeding, clothing, forgiving, nursing, healing and celebrating with your loved ones continue the work begun by Christ.

A reading from the holy gospel according to John
[*Remain in my love.*]

Jesus said to his disciples:
 "As the Father has loved me,

so I have loved you.
Live on in my love.
You will live in my love
if you keep my commandments,
even as I have kept my Father's commandments,
and live in his love.
All this I tell you
that my joy may be yours
and your joy may be complete.
This is my commandment:
love one another
as I have loved you."
This is the gospel of the Lord.

John 15:12–16

Continuing with the same idea as the previous verses, Jesus reminds us that we are his friends when we do as he commands.

Your relationship with God does not begin and end in church. Neither can your love for each other be contained within the bounds of family life. That love extends itself willingly and frequently to others.

A reading from the holy gospel according to John
[*This is my commandment: love one another.*]

Jesus said to his disciples:
"This is my commandment:
love one another
as I have loved you.
There is no greater love than this:
to lay down one's life for one's friends.
You are my friends
if you do what I command you.
I no longer speak of you as slaves,
for a slave does not know what his master is about.

138

Instead, I call you friends,
since I have made known to you all that I heard from
    my Father.
It was not you who chose me,
it was I who chose you
to go forth and bear fruit.
Your fruit must endure,
so that all you ask the Father in my name
he will give you."
This is the gospel of the Lord.

♥

John 17:20–23;
or John 17:20–26

The love of God has existed from before the foundation
of the earth. Jesus prays that we who are united in him may
share always in that perfecting love.

There are many reasons for proclaiming your vows
publicly in church. Whatever those reasons may be, by
asking God's blessing on your union, you are making a
statement about what is significant to you at an important
time in your life. Are you reaffirming your desire to follow
Christ or merely following a family tradition?

A reading from the holy gospel according to John
[May they be completely one.]
(Long Form)

Jesus looked up to heaven and prayed:
    "Holy Father,
    I do not pray for my disciples alone.
    I pray also for those who will believe in me
        through their word,
    that all may be one
    as you, Father, are in me, and I in you,
    I pray that they may be [one] in us,
    that the world may believe that you sent me.

139

I have given them the glory you gave me
that they may be one, as we are one—
I living in them, you living in me—
that their unity may be complete.
So shall the world know that you sent me,
and that you loved them as you loved me.
Father,
all those you gave me
I would have in my company
where I am,
to see this glory of mine
which is your gift to me,
because of the love you bore me before the
    world began.
Just Father,
the world has not known you,
but I have known you;
and these men have known that you sent me
To them I have revealed your name,
and I will continue to reveal it
so that your love for me may live in them
and I may live in them."
This is the gospel of the Lord.

OR
(Short Form)
Jesus looked up to heaven and prayed:
    "Holy Father,
I do not pray for my disciples alone.
I pray also for those who will believe in me
    through their word,
that all may be one
as you, Father, are in me, and I in you,
I pray that they may be [one] in us,
that the world may believe that you sent me.
I have given them the glory you gave me
that they may be one, as we are one—

I living in them, you living in me—
that their unity may be complete.
So shall the world know that you sent me,
and that you loved them as you loved me."
This is the gospel of the Lord.

The Rehearsal

The Rehearsal

Beginning the wedding rehearsal is rather like handing over your ticket for a roller coaster ride. By this time, things are pretty much out of your control. What's done is done. What isn't done probably won't get done and you'll survive the experience anyway. The rehearsal serves to smooth out some of the twists and turns of this most exhilarating ride. All of the passengers, celebrant included, need to be acutely aware of the needs and concerns of others as zero hour rapidly approaches.

Punctuality, always a gesture of respect, is mandatory for both priest and wedding party alike where the rehearsal is concerned. The priest might have a meeting or another rehearsal after yours and will not be able to wait for latecomers. If you have friends who are rarely on time, simply tell them and confirm by mail: "We will gather at the church at 5 p.m." You are not lying to them if the rehearsal doesn't actually begin until 5:30. If they arrive at 5:00, so much the better. They can socialize and take a tour of the church before things get underway.

The wedding party has the right to presume that the rehearsal will begin and end on time so that other festivities will stay on schedule. The groom's dinner should always be after the rehearsal.

Everyone will feel at ease if you arrive early, welcome each one who comes and introduce those who haven't met. It is especially important that everyone is introduced to the priest. Start with your parents. "Fr. Walsh, these are my parents, Stella and Stanley Kowalski, who have just arrived by streetcar from Desire. Mom and Dad, I'd like you to meet Fr. Walsh, our pastor." They will smile, shake hands and say to each other, "I've heard so much about you," which they may interpret any way they like. Then introduce the priest to the members of your wedding party. Even if he doesn't remember all the names, he will remember most of the connections. During the rehearsal, he would like to be able to address your maid of honor as "Meg" or "Jo's sister" or "Miss March" instead of "the one over there with the big blue eyes and the bad perm."

Most of us try to get by with introductions like this: "Molly, Paul. Paul, Molly." You will feel more confident about making new friends and keeping the old if you remember this hot little ettiquette tip: It is customary to address the older person first, introducing him or her to the younger. "Grandpa, this is my best friend, Blanche DuBois. Blanche, this is my grandfather, Richard M. Nixon."

At the appointed time, shepherd your loved ones into the first two pews on one side of the church, welcome them as a group and thank them for helping to make these days so joyous. While everyone is convened and somewhat attentive in the hushed atmosphere of the church, you have the opportunity for last-minute instructions. These should include gentle reminders about restrictions on smoking and drinking in the church, chewing gum during the ceremony, being on time, etc. If it helps, preface these admonitions with, "Fr. Walsh said . . ."

If you would like to begin the rehearsal with a prayer, check with the priest. Otherwise he will do the honors. The wedding prayer on page ix would be suitable and can be personalized to include the bride and the groom.

When you practice the vows, the priest asks, "Will you love and honor each other as husband and wife for the rest of your lives?" There is a strong temptation to slap your thigh, stamp your foot and respond, "No," or "(long pause . . .) I'm thinking." Some will think that this isn't very funny, but don't lose too much sleep over it. Giggling is a time-honored way of releasing tension and does not in any way predict the behavior of the giggler during the actual ceremony. It does, however, slow down the proceedings and should be kept to a minimum. You need to have time to ask the priest those

questions which have plagued you and your mothers in the middle of countless nights.

The priest plays a key role in the launching of a new Christian family. A wise priest will remember that while for him the wedding day is a work day, for you it is as momentous an occasion as his ordination was to him. He will see the rehearsal as an opportunity to work with a wide variety of churched and unchurched Catholics and non-Catholics. It is the perfect time for some friendly, good-natured evangelization.

To folks who have had little exposure to Catholic priests, your celebrant is representing the Church. If you have made every attempt to observe the laws of the parish, etiquette, and common sense, your priest is sure to temper efficiency with grace and good humor. When the rehearsal is over, everyone will be in a good mood and looking forward to the festivities.

The Audience

Guests

Many families report that compiling a guest list for a wedding is only slightly less complicated and more stressful than filling out a federal income tax return.

As far as that goes, the best piece of advice is this: do not, under any circumstances, invite anyone with the assumption that she or he will be unable to attend. As soon as you write a check to the caterer for 279 plates of Beef Wellington with new potatoes and creamed onions, you will get a call from Ginny and Babs, the bride's sorority sisters, who just decided that it would be a gas to fly in from Manitoba. With their husbands. You now have to pick up two more bottles of champagne (Babs always could drink any Alpha Sig under the table) and tell the caterer to open another cow.

Once the list is absolutely final, with all question marks erased, your friends will assume three different roles.

Your friends and family members are considered guests when you plan the rehearsal dinner, the reception or any other purely social function. While thinking of them this way, you may secretly wonder what sort of gift they might choose, how much they will eat and drink, and how they will behave toward one another.

You may think of your friends as spectators when planning your wardrobe, the line-up of your attendants and the color of the horse-drawn carriage that will transport you to the reception, There is little to worry about here. This is one audience sure to give a glowing review.

However, when planning the liturgy, you must consider that your friends are gathering in a church as worshipers, members of a congregation praying together for the first time.

When treating your friends as guests or spectators, you

wouldn't dream of noticing that their religious practices might differ from your own. When thinking of your friends as worshipers, you must recognize and respect diverse backgrounds.

This would not be a problem if you exchanged vows at the 10:00 Mass on a Sunday morning. All assembled would either know the prayers or have a pretty good idea where to find them. They would also anticipate the proper responses and gestures. Drop those faithful Catholics into a Lutheran church some morning. "What? No kneelers? No sign of the cross? Our bodies just don't work this way!"

People unaccustomed to a Catholic liturgy may find themselves distracted by the thought of doing the wrong thing on your important day.

"But," the bride objects, "my family has belonged to Sts. Protect & Preserve Us forever!" That might be true, but it's a safe bet that not all of your friends can make the same claim to fame.

One way to accommodate a non-Catholic bride or groom, prospective in-laws and friends is to exchange vows in a wedding liturgy that does not include a Mass.

Brides and grooms might find this adjustment quite acceptable. Concerned Catholic parents and grandparents, on the other hand, may need to be convinced by the pastor that a sacramental union is, in fact, completed with or without the Eucharist. (See "To Eucharist or Not To Eucharist," p. 93)

As you outline the schedule of events, guests, spectators and worshipers alike should be treated with utmost respect. If you indicate on the invitation that the wedding will begin at 11:30, the wedding should begin at 11:30. If you allow the photographer to delay you for fifteen minutes, then take a long distance call from your twin brother stationed in Peru, then wait for all ten members of the Tuscadaro family (who are always late for everything) to sign the guest book, people will groan rather than grin as you walk down the aisle.

After the wedding, you must get to the reception as

soon as possible. You're tempting fate if you spend another hour with the photographer while your guests spend that same hour at the bar. Having your pictures taken before the wedding eliminates this problem very nicely and gives you something fun to do to unwind a little bit before the liturgy begins.

If you notice the priest or the organist absent from the festivities, you may have forgotten to invite them. Few people attend parties to which they have not been invited. It's too late to think of it when the food is being served, so don't ask the father of the bride or the best man to go knock on doors. During the rehearsal it is too late to invite anyone anywhere. Believe it or not, priests have social lives that go beyond wedding receptions and Knights of Columbus spaghetti dinners. Musicians have families with plans for the rest of the weekend. Be sure to invite *all* guests in plenty of time for them to arrange to join you.

The Receiving Line

One of the most anxiety producing events in all of weddingdom is the receiving line. Even people who are not usually shy tend to blanch at the prospect of greeting a whole church full of people one by one.

Perhaps you have suggested to your intended that you skip the receiving line altogether because you don't want to do it and because it takes time which could be better spent partying at the reception. But in your heart of hearts you know that's not right.

The task is not nearly as difficult as it first appears. Go out right now and get a Powdermilk Biscuit which you undoubtedly have on hand from the folks in Lake Wobegon, Minnesota. This will give you the strength to do the things that have to be done. Greeting your guests individually is one of those things.

Some brides and grooms greet their guests while making the rounds at the reception. This hit and miss approach is chancy because you will miss as many as you hit and probably interrupt some very interesting conversations in the process.

The unavoidable fact is that you have invited all of your guests because you want them to share this festive event with you. Not to greet each one of them personally is worse than a simple social gaffe, and the receiving line is the only sure way to fulfill this obligation.

The following options and suggestions will make it easier.

Though some families attempt to receive guests before the wedding, that time is usually taken up with more important matters like adjusting boutonnieres and bra straps. The more traditional approach is to wait until the ceremony concludes, then line up the principals either at

the door of the church or at the entrance of wherever the
reception will be held.

Some families invite all members of the wedding party,
parents and grandparents, aunts, uncles and their dogs
Phydeaux to stand with them. This is neither practical nor
necessary.

Those hosting the party, and their guests of honor,
receive their guests. This means the bride and groom and
their parents. Period. If there have been remarriages by any
of the parents, consult those intimately involved before
deciding who will greet the guests with you. Don't hesitate
to ask the priest for help or advice.

Who stands where and why?

Protocol dictates that each family member will

introduce friends and relatives to members of the other family. Therefore, no one in the receiving line should stand next to his or her spouse (except for the newlyweds, of course). From left to right you should read like this: bride's mother, groom's father, bride, groom, bride's father, groom's mother. There may be slight variation if there are additional parents due to remarriage.

The supposition that each family member will introduce his or her friends is pious fiction at its best. The reality is that on a wedding day you will have enough trouble remembering your own name let alone the name of the lady who used to help your mother till her garden every spring since you were a baby.

Simply greet each guest with a warm smile, a hug and kiss or a firm handshake and one of the following lines: "How good to see you!" "We're so glad you could join us!" or "Thanks so much for coming!" You need remember only these three lines or reasonable facsimiles thereof. Those passing through the line will hear you say something different to each guest and your breezy self-confidence will put them at ease.

It's not quite over yet. After delivering one of the receiving lines, you then turn to the person next to you in line and say to the guest, "Have you met the father of the groom?" (or whoever it is). Isn't that great? You don't have to remember *anyone's* name! And it's better if you don't even try. Otherwise you are sure to forget that your sister Pat and her new husband (also Pat) have decided to be called Trish and Patrick, and have different last names.

These tips are foolproof and should be shared with all who plan to join you in this demanding task, especially those who assume that it is more demanding than it really is.

You might also remember that there are no enemies at your wedding. These people have accepted your invitation because they want to rejoice with you on this special day. Let them come individually to say how glad they are to share in your happiness!

Part II

Behind the Scenes

How to Get the Most Out of Marriage Prep

It is usually difficult to get married in a Catholic church without at least three months' advance notice. The time between your request and the actual ceremony is not a waiting period but a preparation period. Because Catholic tradition says that you only go around once where marriage is concerned, it is the duty of the Church to see to it that you are as well prepared as possible to make this permanent commitment.

Requirements imposed by your parish or diocese are designed to be helpful, and not a series of hoops through which you must jump, gowned, veiled and tuxed, before you may exchange vows.

Marriage prep varies in form and content depending on where you live. You might have options that range from spending an entire weekend at a retreat house to visiting with your pastor for a few hours.

No matter what type of instruction is available, the same advice you always received about every class you ever took applies here: You get out of it what you put into it.

Here are several suggestions to help make these usually mandatory sessions quite bearable.

First of all, sign up early. Second of all, sign up early. Third of all, sign up early.

If you register as soon as possible after the date is set, you will be guaranteed a spot in the program of your choice.

And you will enjoy it more. Two weeks before the wedding it is impossible to concentrate on communication, conflict resolution, and sacramental grace if the rings don't fit, the airline tickets haven't arrived, and the best man has chicken pox. If you enter into the process of preparing for marriage at least six months before the wedding, you will be able to focus on really important issues like how many Thanksgiving dinners one couple can reasonably be expected to consume in one day.

Another advantage of signing on early is that you will have more time to work on the areas of your relationship that need it. Two weeks before the wedding is not the time to find out that he wants a house filled with kids while she's thinking more along the lines of an apartment and maybe a hamster. With six or more months to go, a wedding can be discreetly delayed if it becomes apparent that there are major differences to be resolved.

Give your marriage prep sessions high priority. Know when you are expected to arrive and how long you are expected to stay. Arrange well in advance to take off work if necessary.

Rather than just one more thing on a long list of things to do, turn it into a date and go out to eat afterward (or before if it's an evening session), either alone or with some of the other couples.

If your partner is reluctant to attend, discuss the reasons for the doubt before you go. There's nothing worse than having to go with a partner who is dead set against the idea.

If you have allowed enough time before the wedding, relax and enjoy the chance to spend some quality time together.

Avoid:

- asking your mother to make the arrangements. You may have thought that graduating from college, getting drunk once, and buying life insurance was sufficient notice to society of your status as an adult. Getting married tops them all, so Mom shouldn't have to do the work.

- complaining about the cost of the program. Considering what you'll spend on flowers, pictures, and all the et ceteras, marriage preparation is cheap at twice the price.

- an unexcused no-show. Whenever you make a reservation for anything, the only acceptable excuse for not calling if you can't come is an unexpected death—yours.

Records and Papers and So On

Catholics do lots of paperwork before they get to the altar. Some of it may seem like busy work to you. Some days it probably seems like that to your pastor, too. All of these steps, however, are taken to safeguard your individual rights and to make clear to you the seriousness of the step you are taking. It really shouldn't be any easier to get married than it is to get papers for your new puppy!

The priest will ask you to get a recently issued copy of your baptismal certificate (that means issued less than six months ago; the souvenir edition in your mother's cedar chest isn't the one you need). If you will be married in the church of your baptism, you can ignore this first piece of paperwork. Those to be married in a parish other than that of their baptism will find that the certificate will be supplied routinely at your request by the pastor of the parish in which you were baptized.

The flip side of the baptismal certificate will indicate that you have not been married and will then serve as a statement of your current freedom to marry. If you really want to impress the priest, arrive at your first interview with baptismal certificate in hand. Simply write or call the church of your baptism, telling them your name, your parents' names (including mom's maiden name), the date of your birth and the approximate date of your baptism. Enclose a self-addressed and stamped envelope for speedier delivery.

Someone baptized in another Christian Church may find it more difficult to get a current certificate. In this case, any proof of baptism will be acceptable.

After your marriage, the church of baptism of the Catholic party will be officially informed and notation of the marriage will be added to your baptismal record.

Catholics are among the world's best record keepers!

You can check out the sample baptismal certificate here to know what kind of document to expect.

The Holy Sacrament of Baptism

This is to certify

That _____

Child of _____

and _____

born in _____
                        City   State

on _____ 19 _____

was Baptized on _____

in the Church of _____

City _____

according to the Roman Rite of the Catholic Church

by the Rev. _____

Sponsors were _____

and _____

as recorded in the Baptismal Register of this church.

Pastor _____

Date _____

Notations

FIRST
COMMUNION

CONFIRMATION

MARRIAGE

ORDINATION

RELIGIOUS
PROFESSION

Affidavit Concerning Marital Freedom

If either or both of you are not known personally by the priest who is assisting you, he may ask for an Affidavit Concerning Marital Freedom. This simply means that he needs from someone who knows you well a statement that you are free to marry.

If he asks you to have the form completed, the witness (a parent, sibling, relative, friend or associate) is asked to bring it to any Catholic priest and have him ask the necessary questions. Both the witness of your choice and the priest sign the form; it is then hit with the Church's seal and is mailed or carried back to the priest who first gave it to you.

A sample of that form follows.

PRIEST ARRANGING MARRIAGE: **WITNESS TO BE INTERVIEWED:**

_____   _____
(Name)   (Name)

_____   _____
(Parish)   (Parish)

_____   _____
(Address)   (City)

Date of Marriage: _____

AFFIDAVIT CONCERNING THE MARITAL FREEDOM OF

_____
(Hereafter referred to as "This Person")

. . . .

Are you related to this person? ___ If so, how? _____

If not, how long and how well do you know this person? _____

_____

Has this person ever been married before (Church or civil)? ___ (If the answer is "Yes", please give the details – number of previous marriage(s), name of former spouse(s), date and place of previous marriage(s), etc.)

_____

_____

Do the parents of this person approve of the forthcoming marriage? _

If not, what is their objection? _____

Do you know of any reason why this person should not be married in the Catholic Church now? ___ If so, why not? _____

Do you know of anything else that should be disclosed in regard to this person's forthcoming marriage? _____

Do you declare that the above answers are the entire truth? _____

SEAL   _____
         (Signature of Witness)

         _____
         (Signature of Priest)

Date: _____

Prenuptial Interview

In addition to the basics of name, address, and dates of birth and baptism, your priest or deacon will also ask you some questions which will indicate your freedom and ability to be married. He'll tell you why he needs to know and what he must ask.

Usually, he will ask these questions of each of you individually so that you have the opportunity to say in privacy that you are entering marriage freely.

He will explain that an impediment is something that would stand in the way of your marriage. If one of you is a priest or nun, for example, you cannot enter a valid, sacramental marriage. Relation by blood is another impediment. In the unlikely event that an impediment exists, the priest will help you to understand how civil or canon law affects you.

A form similar to the one he will complete with you follows.

Prenuptial Interview
The Groom

NAME _____

ADDRESS _____

TELEPHONE _____ BIRTHDATE _____

Is your name as appears above that given at birth? _____

If not, the priest will review the documentation.

Parish to which you belong? _____

Father's name _____

Mother's maiden name _____

What religion do you actively profess? _____

In what religion were you baptized? _____

Confirmed? ___ Yes ___ No

In what church were you baptized? _____
                                        Name and Place

Date of Baptism? _____

For Catholics include certificate issued within past 6 months.

How long have you known your intended spouse? _____

When did you become engaged? _____

Do you have any doubts about entering this marriage? _____

Are you bound by any of the following impediments to marriage?
Vows/Sacred orders (C. 1078) ___ Yes ___ No; Crime (C. 1090) ___ Yes
___ No; Blood Relationship (C. 1091) ___ Yes ___ No; Affinity (C. 1092) ___
Yes ___ No; Public Propriety (C. 1093) ___ Yes ___ No; Legal Relationship
(C. 1094) ___ Yes ___ No

Are you aware of any physical or psychological condition which would
hinder or interfere with your marriage (C. _____

Have you ever attempted or entered a marriage previously? _____

If affirmative, see back page.

Are you placing any conditions on your marriage consent? _____

Are you marrying because of force or fear arising from persons or circumstances? _____

Is there anything else which you should reveal concerning your proposed marriage? _____

I understand that Christian marriage is an irrevocable convenant which is both permanent and indissoluble. I also understand the responsibilities of marriage. Accordingly, I am entering this marriage freely and I intend to be faithful to my spouse.

_____   _____
Signature of Groom   Date

TO BE COMPLETED BY PRIEST/DEACON:
I personally vouch for the freedom to marry of the groom.
__ Yes __ No
Since the groom is unknown to me, a freedom to marry affidavit is included. __ Yes __ No

_____   _____
Signature of Priest/Deacon   Church and Place

The Printing Point, Inc.

650 James Road
Alpharetta, GA 30004
(770) 442-3476

Bridal Sense
404-256-4696
6600 Roswell Rd. NE 30328

Bridals by Lori
6021 Sandy Springs Circle NE
404-252-8767 30328

~~Old~~
Bridesmaids Bow Tique
0595 Old Alabama Rd Ste 21
~~404~~(770) 6401116 30309

Alpharetta, GA

Glad Rags
9850 Nesbit Ferry Rd.
30022 - (770) 992-3134

Bridal Affairs
2016 Hables Ln At, 30350
(678)-320-0144

Prenuptial Interview
The Bride

NAME _____

ADDRESS _____

TELEPHONE _____ BIRTHDATE _____

Is your name as appears above that given at birth? _____

If not, the priest will review the documentation.

Parish to which you belong? _____

Father's name _____

Mother's maiden name _____

What religion do you actively profess? _____

In what religion were you baptized? _____

Confirmed? __ Yes __ No

In what church were you baptized? _____
Name and Place

Date of Baptism? _____

For Catholics include certificate issued within past 6 months.

How long have you known your intended spouse? _____

When did you become engaged? _____

Do you have any doubts about entering this marriage? _____

Are you bound by any of the following impediments to marriage?
Vows/Sacred orders (C. 1078) __ Yes __ No; Crime (C. 1090) __ Yes
__ No; Blood Relationship (C. 1091) __ Yes __ No; Affinity (C. 1092) __
Yes __ No; Public Propriety (C. 1093) __ Yes __ No; Legal Relationship
(C. 1094) __ Yes __ No

Are you aware of any physical or psychological condition which would
hinder or interfere with your marriage (C. _____

Have you ever attempted or entered a marriage previously? _____

If affirmative, see back page.

Are you placing any conditions on your marriage consent? _____

Are you marrying because of force or fear arising from persons or circumstances? _____

Is there anything else which you should reveal concerning your proposed marriage? _____

I understand that Christian marriage is an irrevocable convenant which is both permanent and indissoluble. I also understand the responsibilities of marriage. Accordingly, I am entering this marriage freely and I intend to be faithful to my spouse.

_____   _____
Signature of Bride   Date

TO BE COMPLETED BY PRIEST/DEACON:
I personally vouch for the freedom to marry of the bride. __
Yes __ No
Since the bride is unknown to me, a freedom to marry affidavit is included. __ Yes __ No

_____   _____
Signature of Priest/Deacon   Church and Place

Some Questions When There Has Been A Former Marriage By The Prospective Bride Or Groom

PREVIOUS MARRIAGES OF BRIDE

1. Name of first spouse? _____
   Religion of first spouse? _____
   When did marriage occur? _____
   Was marriage invalid? If so, why? _____
   Who officiated? (*Priest, minister, civil official?*) _____
   Is spouse still living? (*If deceased, attach certificate.*) _____
   Was marriage dissolved by divorce or by Church decree? (*Attach document or decree.*) _____

2. Name of second spouse? _____
   Religion of second spouse? _____
   When did marriage occur? _____
   Was marriage invalid? If so, why? _____
   Who officiated? (*Priest, minister, civil official?*) _____
   Is spouse still living? (*If deceased, attach certificate.*) _____
   Was marriage dissolved by divorce or by Church decree? (*Attach document or decree.*) _____

What obligations do you have toward any previous spouse or children from previous union? _____

PREVIOUS MARRIAGES OF GROOM

1. Name of first spouse? _____
   Religion of first spouse? _____
   When did marriage occur? _____
   Was marriage invalid? If so, why? _____
   Who officiated? (*Priest, minister, civil official?*) _____
   Is spouse still living? (*If deceased, attach certificate.*) _____
   Was marriage dissolved by divorce or by Church decree? (*Attach document or decree.*) _____

2. Name of second spouse? _____
   Religion of second spouse? _____
   When did marriage occur? _____
   Was marriage invalid? If so, why? _____
   Who officiated? (*Priest, minister, civil official?*) _____
   Is spouse still living? (*If deceased, attach certificate.*) _____
   Was marriage dissolved by divorce or by Church decree? (*Attach document or decree.*) _____

What obligations do you have toward any previous spouse or children from previous union? _____

Marriage Between a Catholic and a Baptized Non-Catholic

A Catholic who will marry a baptized non-Catholic requires the permission of the Catholic bishop. This permission is routinely given for the "spiritual welfare of the parties."

A form similar to the one your priest must complete is included here.

Canonical Permission For a Marriage Between a Catholic And Baptized Non-Catholic

By virtue of the faculty granted me by the Bishop of the Diocese of ————————— I hereby grant permission for the marriage between ————————————, a Catholic, and ————————————, a baptized non-Catholic to take place on ———————————— at ————————————.

In accord with Canon 1125, the declaration and promise of the Catholic party have been given.

Canonical reasons for this permission:
———— 1. Spiritual welfare of the parties
———— 2. Well-founded hope that the non-Catholic will enter full communion with the Church
———— 3. Danger of attempted invalid marriage
———— 4. Convalidation
———— 5. Other (Specify): ————————————

—————————————————————

Date	Priest/Deacon

—————————————————————
Church

—————————————————————
City & State

Dispensation from the Impediment of Disparity of Cult

A form similar to the following one is completed when a Catholic plans a marriage to someone who is not baptized. This permission, like the last one, is readily given for the "spiritual welfare of the parties."

Dispensation From The Impediment Of Disparity of Cult (Ad Cautelam)

Note: This form is to be used for the marriage of a Catholic and non-baptized or doubtfully baptized party.

By virtue of the faculty granted me by the Bishop of the Diocese of _____ I hereby grant a dispensation from the impediment of Disparity of Cult (Ad Cautelam) as it exists between _____ , the Catholic party, and _____, the non-baptized or doubtfully baptized party. This marriage will take place on _____ at _____ .

In accord with Canon 1125, the declaration and promise of the Catholic party have been given.

The reason for this request is _____
_____

_____
Date

_____
Priest/Deacon

_____
Church

_____
City & State

Promise of the Catholic Party

In a marriage with a non-Catholic, the Catholic party must promise that children will be raised as Catholics. It should be noted that the Catholic also promises to respect "the conscience of my partner in marriage." The non-Catholic is not asked to make this promise.

A sample declaration and promise follows.

DECLARATION AND PROMISE OF THE CATHOLIC PARTY

I, _____, reaffirm my faith in Jesus Christ and, with God's help, intend to continue living that faith in the Catholic Church. At the same time, I acknowledge the respect I owe to the conscience of my partner in marriage. Therefore, I promise to do all I can to share the faith I have received with our children by having them baptized and educated as Catholics.

STATEMENT OF THE PRIEST/DEACON

The required promise and declaration have been made by the Catholic party in my presence. The non-Catholic party has been informed of this requirement so that it is certain he/she is aware of the promise and obligation on the part of the Catholic party. Both parties are sincere and I am happy to witness their marriage.

Date	**Priest/Deacon**
	Church
	City & State

Petition for Dispensation from the Canonical Form of Marriage

When a Catholic person asks to be married outside of a Catholic church building and in the presence of someone other than a Catholic priest, a form similar to the one that follows is completed by a priest who sends it on to your bishop. This permission is granted for different reasons in different places; ask your priest for the particulars.

With this permission, a marriage contracted outside of a Catholic church is sacramental; without this permission, the Church will not recognize your marriage.

Yes, you're quite correct that this is all very confusing. Your priest will be happy to fill in the blanks.

Petition For Dispensation From The Canonical Form Of Marriage

To be completed by Priest/Deacon and sent to the Marriage Department of the Diocesan Pastoral Center along with Prenuptial Interview.

_____, the Catholic party, who wishes to marry _____, the non-Catholic party, on _____, requests a dispensation from the Canonical Form of Marriage (C. 1108) so that the marriage can take place in _____
Church, Address, City, State

in the presence of _____ .
Name and Denomination

The reason for this request is _____

_____

_____	_____
Date	Priest/Deacon
	_____
	Church
	_____
	City & State

Most Frequently Asked Questions and Their Answers

QUESTION: What about marriages between two Christians of different denominations—a Catholic and a Lutheran, for example. If the wedding is in a Catholic church, can you invite the minister from the Lutheran church to be part of the ceremony?

Usually, yes. Most priests are quite good about inviting the participation of another minister. Some will invite the visitor to say a prayer, pronounce a blessing, read from scripture or preach the homily. Much will depend on the custom in your town.

♥

QUESTION: Can a Catholic be married in a non-Catholic church?

Sometimes. If, for example, a Catholic man wants to marry a non-Catholic woman and promises to baptize and raise the children as Catholics, it is possible that the wedding ceremony can take place in her church with her minister presiding and witnessing the vows. The technical term for this is dispensation from form, and it means that the traditional Catholic ceremony can sometimes be replaced by a ceremony of another sort. This dispensation or permission must come from your bishop, but the request is made through your pastor. Visit with him if you have questions and he'll tell you what is possible in your area.

♥

QUESTION: What if a Catholic person who has never married wants to marry a Lutheran who was married to another Lutheran in a Lutheran church?

Always presume that a marriage entered into by two Protestant people is a valid bond. For a more complete answer in this and any similar instance, call your pastor or the marriage tribunal which usually has an office in the chancery or bishop's office.

♥

QUESTION: What happens if I disregard the Church laws about marriage or remarriage?

If your marriage is not recognized by the Church, you are still bound to worship as a Catholic person, but cannot receive the sacraments. You are not excommunicated but are in an irregular situation. A priest can explain to you how you can explore or begin the process of reconciling with the Church.

♥

QUESTION: What about having our wedding during Lent?

This is generally not a good idea. Lent is a time of penance and preparation for Easter. The festivity of a wedding feast is usually thought to be inappropriate to the season.

♥

QUESTION: Is it a good idea to chew gum during the wedding as a way to keep down the anxiety level?

No!

♥

Rite Of Catholic Marriage Within Mass

Prior to the ceremony: music

Parents are seated

Processional: ⎯⎯⎯⎯⎯⎯⎯⎯⎯⎯⎯⎯⎯⎯⎯⎯⎯

When the bridal party has entered the sanctuary, HYMN:

⎯⎯⎯⎯⎯⎯⎯⎯⎯⎯⎯⎯⎯⎯⎯⎯⎯⎯⎯⎯⎯⎯⎯⎯⎯⎯⎯

Greeting, welcome, opening prayer.

Old Testament reading: ⎯⎯⎯⎯⎯⎯⎯⎯⎯⎯⎯⎯⎯

Psalm (sung by congregation or soloist): ⎯⎯⎯⎯⎯

New Testament: ⎯⎯⎯⎯⎯⎯⎯⎯⎯⎯⎯⎯⎯⎯⎯⎯⎯

Gospel: ⎯⎯⎯⎯⎯⎯⎯⎯⎯⎯⎯⎯⎯⎯⎯⎯⎯⎯⎯⎯⎯

Homily

Exchange of vows: ⎯⎯⎯⎯⎯⎯⎯⎯⎯⎯⎯⎯⎯⎯⎯

Blessing and exchange of rings

Hymn or solo: ⎯⎯⎯⎯⎯⎯⎯⎯⎯⎯⎯⎯⎯⎯⎯⎯⎯

Preface: ⎯⎯⎯⎯⎯⎯⎯⎯⎯⎯⎯⎯⎯⎯⎯⎯⎯⎯⎯⎯

Acclamations during the Eucharistic prayer:

Holy, Holy: ⎯⎯⎯⎯⎯⎯⎯⎯⎯⎯⎯⎯⎯⎯⎯⎯⎯⎯

Memorial Acclamations: ⎯⎯⎯⎯⎯⎯⎯⎯⎯⎯⎯⎯

Great Amen: ⎯⎯⎯⎯⎯⎯⎯⎯⎯⎯⎯⎯⎯⎯⎯⎯⎯

Lord's Prayer, recited or sung by entire congregation.

Nuptial Blessing ⎯⎯⎯⎯⎯⎯⎯⎯⎯⎯⎯⎯⎯⎯⎯⎯

Communion hymn ⎯⎯⎯⎯⎯⎯⎯⎯⎯⎯⎯⎯⎯⎯⎯⎯

Blessing and dismissal of congregation

Recessional: ⎯⎯⎯⎯⎯⎯⎯⎯⎯⎯⎯⎯⎯⎯⎯⎯⎯⎯

Rite Of Catholic Marriage
Outside Of Mass

Prior to the ceremony: music (if desired)

Parents are seated

Processional: _____

When the bridal party has entered the sanctuary, HYMN:

_____

Greeting, welcome, opening prayer.

Old Testament reading: _____

Psalm (sung by congregation or soloist): _____

Second Reading: _____

Gospel: _____

Homily

Exchange of vows, blessing and exchange of rings

Hymn or solo (for hymn, see options above for opening hymns).

_____

Lord's Prayer, recited or sung by entire congregation.

Nuptial Blessing _____

Blessing and dismissal of congregation

Recessional: _____

Part III

Beyond the Footlights

Copy and Carry:
The Best Man's Duties

Before the Ceremony:

- Be certain that at all pre-wedding festivities there is a driver available who has refrained from alcohol and all other debilitating substances.
- Run interference for the groom so that he does not find himself in any situation that might hinder him in his ability to function on the wedding day.
- If you are entrusted with the rings, see that they arrive at the church when you do and are safely kept in your pants' pocket until they are called for. (Take them out of the jeweler's box first.) Don't wear the rings on your own fingers; they are too easily lost or stuck.
- Get the offering for the priest from the groom and keep it in your jacket pocket.

During the Rehearsal:

- Help get everyone involved into position so that the rehearsal can begin at the appointed hour.
- Find out when and where you will be expected to sign the marriage license.

During the Ceremony:

- Be attentive to the priest in the event that he calls expectedly or unexpectedly for your assistance.
- Be solicitous to the groom in the hour of his great nervousness.

After the Ceremony:

- Be available at the requested moment to sign the marriage license.
- Thank the priest for his kindness (even if you weren't moved by any particular display of feeling) and offer him the envelope which you were given before the games began. When handing him the envelope, you might say, "Bunny and Claude want you to have this." Do not say, "Here's a little something for your trouble."
- Go to the reception and worry about having to propose the first toast which you have written or borrowed in advance and which you have already practiced several times. If you're not feeling creative, you can borrow this one: "To Ralph and Wanda: may they live long and prosper!"

The Maid or Matron of Honor's Duties

Before the Ceremony:

- Be certain that at all pre-wedding festivities there is a driver available who has refrained from alcohol and all other debilitating substances.
- Assist the bride in any situations which may hinder her from getting to the church on time.

At the Rehearsal:

- Work with the best man to see that all who have a part in the action are ready at the appointed time in the proper place.
- Ask if, when and where you are to sign the marriage license.

During the Ceremony:

- Be attentive to the bride. Be sure you know where the Kleenex is.

After the Ceremony:

- Be ready to sign the marriage license as requested.
- Proceed with all appropriate haste to the next appointed place.

The Reader's Duties

At the Rehearsal:

- Practice, using the microphone, the scripture readings which you have already read at home so often that they are almost memorized.
- Reconcile yourself to the translation of the scripture which has been established for use. Don't ad lib a new translation because you will most probably end up with mismatched subjects and verbs.
- Note that the translation in this book is the same as you will find at the church. Ask for a copy of these readings to practice with rather than using your own Bible or any other source.
- Make sure you know where you will sit during the ceremony and what your cue is to begin reading.
- Ask whether you will carry the book in the entrance procession or find it already at the pulpit.

Before the Ceremony:

- Check to see that the book and microphone and your appointed chair are where you were told at the rehearsal to expect them. If it seems that the microphone has not been turned on, ask the priest.
- Make sure that the reading glasses you brought are yours and not Clarence's or Betty's.

During the Ceremony:

- Watch for the cue you have been given and read with relish at the appointed moment.

- Do not say, "The first reading is a reading from . . . ", but announce very simply what the lectionary provides by way of introduction, "A reading from the Book of . . . "
- When you have concluded, pause and then look at the assembly as you say, "This is the Word of the Lord."

After the Ceremony:

- Accept compliments with gracious thanks.

The Ushers' Duties

At the Rehearsal:

- Arrive on time and be attentive to the requests and directions of the priest, bride, groom and mother of the bride.
- Ask where family members will be seated for the ceremony.
- Find the telephone that will be available for emergency use before or during the ceremony.

Before the Ceremony:

- Be at the church no less than forty-five minutes before the ceremony (unless parish policy calls for a different timetable) dressed and ready to go.
- Use the bathroom now because you'll be too busy even to think about it for quite some time.
- Be ready to assist the priest in moving sanctuary furniture or placing plants and candles.
- See that the aisle runner is securely placed at the head of the aisle and is ready to be unrolled.
- Invite the guests already seated in the back pews to come closer: "Friend, come higher! It's a large church [they're *all* large churches, even the small ones]; you'll see and hear better closer up. Will you follow me, please?"
- Offer your arm to female guests, who are followed by male guests, and lead them to their seats. Place your hand on

the designated pew, step to one side and allow them to be seated. Female ushers do not offer their arm, but walk beside the female guests.

- Assume that all guests are friends of both the bride and groom; divide the guests evenly between the sides of the church unless you are told differently.

- After the aisle seats are filled, seat the guests by the side aisles. And use your head: if the church has fifty pews on each side but only one hundred and twenty guests are expected, direct the guests to pews near the front.

- Note that the left side (where there might be a statue of Mary) as you enter is the bride's side where her family will sit. The right side (where there may be a statue of Joseph) is the groom's side.

- Seat the grandparents of the groom, the grandparents of the bride, the parents of the groom (if they are not in the procession) and, lastly, the mother of the bride (if she is not in the procession). Remember: the groom's family sits facing the male statue; the bride's family sits facing the statue of Mary.

- Ask late arriving guests to wait in the vestibule until the procession has reached the sanctuary. Remove the guest book, if it has been placed in the vestibule, so that late arrivers can be seated without forming a line at the book. See that the book is given to its attendant who will request at the reception signatures of those who may not have signed already.

- Roll the carpet down the aisle, checking to see that no major wrinkles will impede the procession. If there is a tube or rope that needs to be ditched, don't put it in the traffic pattern.

- After the procession, seat the late-comers by the side aisles.

During the Ceremony

- Do not desert the church at any time during the ceremony. If the priest asks for help or to have the windows opened, respond quickly.
- If any guest needs a phone, show him or her where you discovered it to be during the rehearsal.
- If the runner wrinkles or bunches up, straighten it.
- Unless called into service, sit near the back of the church where you can see and be seen.

After the Ceremony

- If the bride wants to keep the plastic runner for covering her tomato plants, save it in the place she specified. If it is disposable, dispose of it. If it is to be returned to the rental shop, put it in the car trunk of whosoever will return it later.
- Dispose of all flower boxes, garment bags and miscellaneous trash.
- Be available to move sanctuary furniture and plants to their permanent homes.
- Sweep up and dispose of rice that may have been thrown
- Check with the priest to see that all details have been attended to.
- Straighten your tie, breathe a sigh of relief over an important job well done and proceed to the reception

Guidelines for Wedding Photographers

A wedding is a religious event. In keeping with the dignity of the sacrament and with reverence for the house of the church in which the marriage takes place, the following guidelines are proposed:

1. The church is not a studio. Photographers are not to move sanctuary furniture (e.g., the altar, pulpit or presider's chair).

2. There should be no disruption or disturbance of the ceremony by the photographer. Use of flash during the ceremony is forbidden.

3. Photographs taken from the back of the church or the balcony are acceptable. They may be taken, without flash, at any time during the ceremony.

4. Use of church facilities is permitted one hour and fifty minutes before the ceremony. The final twenty minutes of this period, at a minimum, is to be left for the bride and groom as a quiet time before the ceremony. The photographer has ninety minutes before the ceremony and may use the church up to one hour after the receiving line has ended.

Parish or diocesan policies take precedence over these guidelines.

These guidelines are adapted from those of the St. Cloud Deanery in the Diocese of St. Cloud in Minnesota.

The Payment Equation Worksheet

What size gift to give to the Church for getting you to the altar? Not too difficult. Use one of the following examples to compute your gift:

A Modest Gift:

(Cost of groom's wedding outfit)
+ (cost of cake)
divided by 2
= gift to church ($_____)

A Generous Gift:

(Cost of bride's wedding clothes)
+ (cost of photography)
divided by 2
= gift to church ($_____)

Sample Programs

THE WEDDING CELEBRATION
Kathleen Marie Kuyava and John Howard Lofstuen
St. Michael's Church

Processional	"Trumpet Voluntary," Purcell
Opening Prayer	
Old Testament Reading	Genesis 2:18–24
Responsorial Psalm	"On Eagle's Wings" Glory & Praise Hymnal, Vol. 2, #126
New Testament Reading	1 John 4:7–12
Gospel	John 15:9–12
Homily	
Exchange of Vows	
Blessing and Exchange of Rings	
Vocal Solo	"One Hand, One Heart"
"Holy, Holy, Holy"	Worship, #253
Memorial Acclamation	#254
Great Amen	#255
The Lord's Prayer	
Nuptial Blessing	
Communion Song	Lights of the City
Final Blessing	
Recessional	"Wedding March," Mendelssohn
Parents of the Bride	*Anne and Gene Kuyava*
Parents of the Groom	*Janet Lofstuen* *John Lofstuen*
Maid of Honor	*Julie Ann Meyer*
Best Man	*David Mount*

Bridesmaids	*Kim Gaida*
	Jennie Wabrowetz
	Linda Ramsey
	Linda Barnstorf
Groomsmen	*Bill Kirsh*
	Bub Kuyava
	Mark Kuyava
	Wayne Gatlin
Ushers	*Greg Kuyava*
	Keith Swanson
	Steve Wabrowetz
Presider	*William Graham*
Reader	*Patrick Murray*
Servers	*Tommy Ernst*
	Kevin Ernst
Organist	*Marie Rock*
Soloist	*Barbara Storms*
Personal Attendants	*Judy Larson*
	Katie Chesness

♥   ♥   ♥

THE WEDDING CELEBRATION
Donna Lou Hardesty and Steven Robert Peterson
St. Michael's Church

Prelude	Soloist
Processional	"Trumpet Voluntary," Purcell
Opening Prayer	
Old Testament Reading	Genesis 2:18–24
Responsorial Psalm	Psalm 33
	Worship Hymnal, No. 36
New Testament Reading	1 John 4:7–12
Gospel	John 15:9–12
Homily	
Exchange of Vows,	
Blessing and Exchange of Rings	
Hymn	"The Lord's Prayer"
Nuptial Blessing	
Final Blessing	
Recessional	"Wedding March," Mendelssohn
Parents of the Bride	*Bill Hardesty*
	Karen and Dick Raun
Parents of the Groom	*Doris and Bob Peterson*
Maid of Honor	*Becky Richardson*
Best Man	*Tom Leider*
Bridesmaids	*Sarah Leischke*
	Janet Wiedemann
Groomsmen	*Tom Kuberra*
	Mike Kuberra
Ushers	*Mike Peterson*
	Craig Peterson
Presider	*Fr. William Graham*
Reader	*Anne Kuyava*
Organist	*Marie Rock*
Soloist	*Julie Adams*
Personal Attendant	*Sheri Johnson*

Rite Of Catholic Marriage Within Mass

Prior to the ceremony: music

Parents are seated

Processional: _____

When the bridal party has entered the sanctuary, HYMN:

_____

Greeting, welcome, opening prayer.

Old Testament reading: _____

Psalm (sung by congregation or soloist): _____

New Testament: _____

Gospel: _____

Homily

Exchange of vows, blessing and exchange of rings

Hymn or solo: _____

Acclamations during the Eucharistic prayer:

Holy, Holy: _____

Memorial Acclamations: _____

Great Amen: _____

Lord's Prayer, recited or sung by entire congregation.

Nuptial Blessing _____

Blessing and dismissal of congregation

Recessional: _____

Rite Of Catholic Marriage
Outside Of Mass

Prior to the ceremony: music (if desired)

Parents are seated

Processional: _____

When the bridal party has entered the sanctuary, HYMN:

_____

Greeting, welcome, opening prayer.

Old Testament reading: _____

Psalm (sung by congregation or soloist): _____

Second Reading: _____

Gospel: _____

Homily

Exchange of vows, blessing and exchange of rings

Hymn or solo (for hymn, see options above for opening hymns).

_____

Lord's Prayer, recited or sung by entire congregation.

Nuptial Blessing _____

Blessing and dismissal of congregation

Recessional: _____